Youth Soccer

Dribbling Skills and

Drills

Chest Dugger

Table Of Contents

ABOUT THE AUTHOR

Chest Dugger is a soccer fan, former professional and coach, looking to share his knowledge. Enjoy this book and several others that he has written.

DISCLAIMER

INTRODUCTION - THE IMPORTANCE OF DRIBBLING

The stocky but diminutive figure picks the ball up just inside his own half, receiving a neat ten-meter pass played with the outside of the foot. Given the danger this man represents, he has been allowed more space than was probably in the game plan. However, as the ball falls under his control, two players descend on him, textbook style, one in front: one behind.

His first touch knocks the ball half a yard towards his own goal, while a little skip denies that foul that would have ended the attack before it started. Now he is facing the second defensive midfielder, but a hop, a drag back and a 180-degree turn sees him heading off towards the halfway line, the two defenders trailing in his wake.

Now he knocks the ball further ahead and accelerates into the opposition half, two touches and he has slipped inside the full back, one more and he is through the gap between the center half and this now trailing defender. Looking back on the TV footage of the time, of those two midfielders, one is now completely out of shot, having given up the ghost, the second was positioned two meters nearer to his goal when the attacker had first received the ball. Now, despite the dribbler having accelerated wide, cut in and bypassed two defenders as though they were not there, that chasing midfield has lost eight or ten meters on his target.

Now the striker dips into the box. With a change of pace and a feint the onrushing keeper, probably the best in the world at the time, is left stranded on his backside. The full back has not given up though, and slides in making a last desperate attempt to prevent the inevitable.

But the striker is as strong as an ox, and the impact of the full back barely makes him shudder. Instead, despite the importance of the occasion, despite the fact his lungs must have been burning, despite the urge bursting through him to blast the ball into the empty net, he side foots it carefully home, Now he wheels away to celebrate what is still widely regarded as the greatest ever solo goal. Not just in World Cup history, but in the history of association football.

Five players have made a total of seven attempted tackles on the striker, none have even touched the ball. Those that got near enough to make contact with the player have bounced off him. A professional running back having fun playing with a gang of ten-year olds. Except this running back has had the ball at his feet, not in his hand.

The scorer is, of course, the irrepressible Diego Maradona, the game, Argentina v England in the 1986 World Cup. During that astonishing run Diego Maradona seems to have written a book about the skills of dribbling. He has evoked the excitement a thrilling dribble brings to the crowd. He has demonstrated how an individual running at a defense can disrupt the most organized of formations. He has displayed an excellent first touch, a range of individual skills (a turn, running with the ball, a feint, a change of pace, dribbling inside and outside tacklers and the ability to stay calm and controlled at the finish). He has run with speed and with perfect balance, while his touch running at speed has been so perfect that never has he had to break stride. Despite running further than his original attempted tackler, and with the ball, he has left him for dead. Remember also, it is 1986 – the pitch is good although far from perfect. At one point, as he cuts inside, the ball bobbles frighteningly, yet Maradona just absorbs the unexpected bounce and continues forward. Such is his balance, so low is his center of gravity that he is both able to avoid lunging tackles, and when contact is made absorb it without losing any control of the ball.

End of book. If only we all had the skills of a Maradona at the top of his game. Yet although we are unlikely to get there, as are the players we coach (if that is our role in soccer), we can become better dribblers; we can apply coaching tips and employ dribbling drills which improve this element of our game, and that of our players.

Aficionados of soccer will know, of course, that Maradona scored two goals in that World Cup match. The other, his first, is equally famous but for far less admirable reasons. It too involved some excellent close skills, a great turn, the beating of a couple of players through the middle and an incisive lay off and run. It was the finish that made the goal infamous though. The 'Hand of God Goal', Maradona's left hand reaching out, fist to the fore, to punch the ball past the outrunning Peter Shilton, England's keeper. (The two have never spoken to this day, thirty-four years later.)

But as a dribbler, with his balance, speed, touch and strength, many agree that Maradona is without peer. There have been other great dribblers over time, of course. In the modern game, Lionel Messi's mesmerizing touch and change of pace stands out. His great rival, Ronaldo, too began his career on the wing, where his pace and touch, allied to one of the best step overs in the history of the game, helped to make him a modern great.

Dribblers come in different forms; players like Johann Cruyff and Zinedine Zidane were blessed with astonishing touch and skills; we will look at the 'turns' named after them later in the book. Thierry Henry, the former France, Arsenal and Barcelona striker was blessed with astonishing pace, and would beat defenders with pure speed, while his eye for a finish made him one of the most prolific goal scorers of all time, notably through his trademark score. Here he would dribble in from the left, using his pace and strength to leave full backs and center halves struggling in his wake. Then, Henry would open his body up before curling a right footed shot away from the keeper and into the bottom corner.

Further back, we can recall the incredible balance of George Best, the brilliance of the Brazilians of the 1960s and early 70s, Jairzinho and Pele, not forgetting players such as Eusebio, Matthews and so on.

What these players have in common is the ability to lift fans to their feet, to provide the excitement a mazy run brings, to make soccer come alive. Let's learn some of the ways they managed to produce these wonderous thrills.

How Strong Dribbling Skills Can Give You an Edge

It is probably truer today than ever that the game is made for dribblers. Firstly, we play on pitches that are so much better than they used to be. 4G technology means we have AstroTurf like the best laid grass, while outdoor grass pitch technology means drainage is maximized and wear minimized.

On top of those physical conditions lending themselves to a dribbling game, defensive tactics are improved to such an extent that even weaker teams can compete with much stronger ones and hold the hope of keeping their more talented opponents from scoring. At all levels players are fitter, and coaches are better. Teams, even youth ones, are more organized.

In order to break down a tough opposition, the need for individual brilliance grows. The superb shot, the defense splitting pass, the brilliantly worked set piece. And, of course, the individual skills of the dribbler.

So, having a team of players (including, to some extent, the keeper) who can dribble increases the opportunity of finding those game changing moments in a match. Strong defensive organization deny the two elements of soccer which show off any player at their best. Time and space. When we have these aspects of the game, our passing, our decision making, our touch and our shooting all improve. It is inevitable that we will find it harder to perform these skills when we are under pressure.

A good dribbler creates that space and time for their teammates. They stretch defenses; they draw players out of position. It is the reason what the traditional 4-4-2 formation is less and less popular, with teams opting for 4-3-3 or 4-2-3-1 formations; organizations which allow for wide players to have the opportunity to dribble, to challenge defenses, to pull their organization apart.

It is probably fair to say that the best dribblers need two broad characteristics:

- Firstly, and less importantly at youth level, are physical attributes.

    - A bit of pace, but where that is lacking, we can teach and practice tricks and acceleration which can give our players the same kinds of advantages as the quickest players.

    - A low center of gravity – again, we can teach balance and body position

    - Two footedness.

- Secondly, and the aspect which we can all acquire, and coaches can instill in every one of their players: practice and technique.

A great way to start is to use dribbling drills as simple warm ups with our youth teams. Good warm ups are simple, they are used regularly so the young players can get on with them quickly without the need for lengthy exposition.

Here are some starter drills and tips some of which might seem so obvious that they do not need stating. But soccer is a simple game, so there is absolutely nothing wrong (indeed, with youngsters, much that is good), about using simple drills. More, it is often the most obvious that eludes our memories.

A Note on Drill Diagrams: Some of the following 100 tips and drills include diagrams to make understanding the drill easier. The following key is applied:

- *Large White Circle – Offensive Player*
- *Large Black Circle – Defensive Player*
- *Large Black or White Circle with G – Goalkeeper*
- *Large Grey Circle – Third Team/Coach/Neutral Player*
- *Black Box with SG – Small Goal*
- *Black Box with BG – Same size Goal as Main Goal*
- *Small Black Circle – Ball*
- *Unfilled White Box - Grid*
- *Small White Triangle – Cone*
- *Small Stick Man – Mannequin*
- *White Arrow – direction of player movement*
- *Black Arrow – direction of ball movement (Note, where a white arrow is next to a black one, this indicates the ball is being dribbled).*

- *Very occasionally, and always noted, we have varied the colors for the sake of clarity.*

Tip and Drill Number One: Dribbling Warm Up (1)

*A good warm up performs a twin function; it must deliver its key aim, which is to warm up muscles and ligaments to reduce the risk of injury. However, there are many ways of doing that. The **best soccer warm ups ALWAYS involve use of a ball**; that way skills are being practised whilst muscles are loosened up.*

Tip and Drill Number Two: Dribbling Warm Up (2)

We want warm ups to be quick to organize and easy for students. This drill, and the next, fulfil all criteria.

Dribbling Aim: To run in a straight line with the ball without breaking stride.

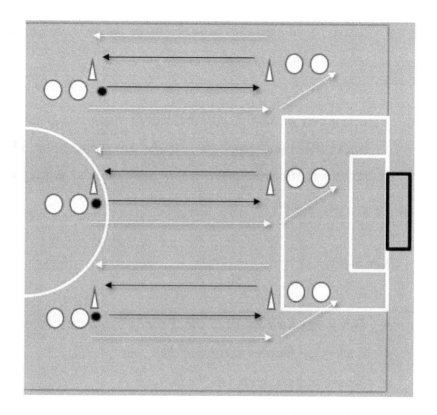

Equipment: One ball each.

Method:

- *Set up a track approximately 25m long (older players could use the width of the pitch, younger ones the width of the penalty areas).*

- *Divide the players into twos and place the twos opposite each other at either end of the track.*

- *One player from each pair dribbles from either end across the track. When they reach the end, the next player goes. There is plenty of action and movement in this drill, and its simplicity allows the coach to be setting up the next drill.*

Key Skills:

- *Encourage the players to knock the ball with their laces.*
- *Encourage players to run 'on their toes'.*
- *Ensure players keep their heads up.*
- *Start at half pace and encourage players to increase their speed with each run.*

Tip and Drill Number Three: Dribbling Warm Up (3)

Dribbling Aim: Add in close control to basic running with the ball. Use both feet.

Equipment: One ball between two; cones laid out along same track as before. The middle cone is a different color to the remainder.

Method:

1) *Divide players into groups of about 6, using the same track as in the previous drill.*

2) *Space each group out along ONE side of the track.*

3) *Player one dribbles between the cones, using both feet to propel the ball in as straight a line as possible.*

4) *When the player reaches the different colored cone, the next player sets off.*

5) *At the end, the player turns and runs with the ball alongside the cones, using the skills developed in the first warm up.*

6) *When the middle cone is reached, the ball is passed with the instep firmly along the ground to the next waiting player, who sets off. The passer then rejoins the end of the line. When running well, four of the six players are in movement, the other two waiting and recovering.*

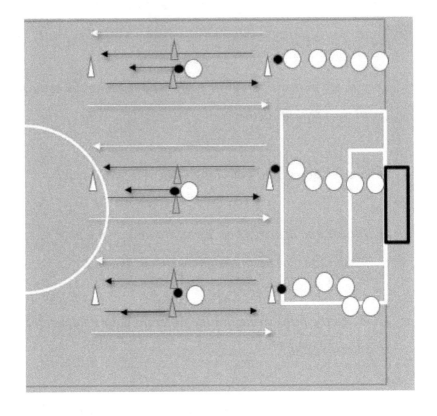

(Note, in the diagram above dribbling/passing is as in the description.)

Key Skills:

1) *Head up.*
2) *Control the ball close to the body.*
3) *Use both the instep and outside of the boot to propel the ball.*
4) *Run with the ball using the laces.*
5) *Pass with the instep.*

Tip and Drill Number Four: Improving Balance (1)

Low Level Pirates: Again, a fun game which kids will love. Keep to low levels, no more than knee high, to avoid injury. This works well indoors, but for those who do not have access to such facilities, is a good game to play on grass or astro.

Use a penalty area, or if indoors, the size of the playing area.

Dribbling Aim: Improve balance

Equipment: Bibs to identify 'pirates'; large number of cones, bibs, hoops etc. to mark out 'land'

Method:

1) *Mark out a playing area by creating spaces with cones, hoops, bibs and so forth which are identified as 'land'. Players may only step or rest on these. It must be possible to get from one piece of 'land' to another,*
2) *Choose two players to be pirates. Their aim is to 'tag' the other players. Once tagged, a player is 'out'.*
3) *If a player steps on the sea, they are out. If a pirate steps on the sea, all the 'out' players are allowed back in.*

4) *Play each round for about two minutes, then change the*
   pirates.

Key Skills: Have fun! Balance will improve as a result.

Tip and Drill Number Five: Improving Balance (2)

Walking football: young players love games with 'silly' aspects
to them. (Actually, so do adults, but that is outside our terms of
reference for this coaching book.). Walking football slows down the
game and allows the coach to put in restrictions which can help with
balance.

Dribbling Aim: Improve balance.

Equipment: Small pitch, for example, half a normal pitch.

Method:

1) *Only walking allowed.*

2) *Sideways walking (for lateral movement, with no crossing of*
   feet), heel to toe walking (for forward movement) only
   allowed.

*3) Play a normal game with only walking allowed. First goal
wins are often enough for this drill*

Key Skills:

1) Arms for balance.

2) Move slowly and with control.

Tip and Drill Number Six: Developing a Low Center of Balance

Tightrope Races: This is a fun way to start or end a session, and
although it doesn't involve a ball, will help young people concentrate
on keeping their core balance straight and low, which will help their
center of balance.

Dribbling Aim: Keep center of gravity low.

*Equipment: Poles, such as corner posts but not with pointed ends
(safety!), narrow tracks such as with squashy cones or narrow planks of
wood.*

Method:

1)   This can work as a relay race, or an individual timed event, where you run from one end to another holding the pole.

2)   Players hold the pole like a tightrope walker, using it to help keep their balance.

3)   They race along their 'track'; if they step off, they must start again.

Key Skills:

1)   Keep low.

2)   Keep the pole even on each side.

3)   Move under control.

Tip and Drill Number Seven: Walking Hopscotch

Kids are usually less easily embarrassed than adults, particularly younger ones. Use this attribute to make opportunities for practicing soccer techniques. Walking hopscotch involves using pavement cracks to develop dexterity. Encourage players to set themselves challenges while walking on the pavement. Ideas can include:

- *Hop from one foot to the other when crossing a pavement crack.*
- *Feint towards one slab but move to the other.*
- *Step with alternate feet from one slab to the next, using arms to maintain balance.*
- *Youngsters are great at coming up with their own 'hopscotch' challenges!*

The Best Positions on the Field to Dribble

We want all of our players to be able to dribble the ball. With young players, it is more important to develop key skills, to allow them to make on-pitch decisions, than to win. This point should be born in mind when players go on a dribble. Do encourage them to express themselves.

However, there are other skills in the game, notably passing, and it can be a fault of young players, who are developmentally still at the 'egotist' stage, to dribble when passing is a better option.

Best Three Areas to Dribble

We dribble to create space by drawing defenders out of position. This can be particularly effective in the following situations:

- When in a wide position, to draw a wide defender out of position, and thus cause a more central player to cover, creating space in the dangerous central area of the pitch.

- From the back, to draw the first line of defense (often the opposing strikers) out of position to create more space for the skilled passers of the midfield.

- On the break, following transition of possession, to allow a team mate to get into a dangerous position and for support to arrive. An early pass is also dangerous but can leave the receiver isolated if the break is particularly quick.

Always on the look out to give our readers a free bonus, we will offer a fourth area to consider, which is in the opposing penalty box.

While on this occasion, dribbling might slow down an attack, allowing the defense to get back in numbers, if not in an organized way (remember, the ball travels faster than a player…) it is the case that defenders are wary of tackling in the penalty box, as an error can lead to a penalty.

Riskiest Places to Dribble

Dribbling is always slightly risky; the risk of being tackled is ever present. The riskiest dribbles occur not in a particular place, but when losing possession can cause risk to our own goal. Thus, losing the ball in our own penalty area is more dangers than in the opposition's, but that does not necessarily mean we should never dribble in our own penalty area. Equally, when a lot of players have committed forward, a central area dribble can be risky as the team is exposed to a rapid transition, for which they are not organized, if possession is lost.

Tip and Drill Number Eight: Don't Listen to Dad; 'Never Dribble in Your Own Box.Half…Give it to Jimmy!'

The world is a more tolerant and inclusive place than it used to be, mostly, and so is the soccer pitch. Dads and mums, grandads and uncles can often hold old fashioned views of the game. We all know the sort of thing: 'Don't pass across your own penalty area', 'don't dribble in your own box', 'defenders shouldn't cross the halfway line,' and so on.

Added to this occasional misunderstanding of good coaching, the sort of fan who feels it is their role to coach from the touchline is likely to be the sort of myopic person who sees their own child as the only player on the pitch with even a modicum of quality. Thus, the instruction of 'Give it to Jimmy,' will often ring out, leading to heavy criticism of (poor) Jimmy when he fails to score from the half way line, or of any player who instead passes to a team mate in a better position.

Such parents know little about soccer, and even less about coaching. They are trying to get their own vicarious joy through their child, to compensate for their own deficiencies.

We might not share such a coruscating assessment of a Dad with our Under Ten team, but we should always tell our teams, order them indeed, **that they only ever listen to four voices on the soccer pitch:**

- *The referee's voice.*
- *Their teammates' voices.*
- *Their coach's voice and...*
- *The voice in their own head.*

With all of this basic knowledge in place, let us move on with tips and drills to make our young players into ever better dribblers.

DRIBBLING FOR TACTICAL ADVANTAGE

When to Dribble...and When to Pass

How many times do we watch games of soccer played at the highest level on TV, only to hear the exasperated voice of the commentator tell us that the player in possession passed too late, or took the wrong option, or should have dribbled it further before passing?

How many times have we watched strikers flap their hands in frustration when a pass is delivered too late, and they have run into an offside position? Or, a dribbling winger has cut inside and lost the ball in seeking a shooting opportunity for themselves, instead of making a simple pass?

And watched a center-half breaking out of defence, only to be tackled and leave their side vulnerable to transition? So, if professional players at the top of their game frequently make wrong decisions, it is hardly likely that our youth teams will avoid such mistakes.

Indeed, in any field (sports, professional, social – life itself), one must make errors in order to learn from them and improve. This is the tenet that runs through this section of our dribbling book. We urge coaches not to forget it.

Tip and Drill Number Nine: Decision Making

So, this tip is an easy one, but nonetheless crucial. **Reward decision making, even if that decision is wrong.** *The best coaches are able to make these rewards genuine, whilst also encouraging young players to review whether or not they made the best decision in the circumstances.* **This self-analysis can only be established in an environment where mental pressure and criticism are the rarest of visitors.**

Tip and Drill Number Ten: Small Goal Rondo Drill

This is a great drill for getting lots of players involved and for encouraging decision making in a semi-pressured situation.

Dribbling Aim: Beat a defender to score.

Equipment: Large area, such as half a junior pitch, or zone marked out 30m x 20m minimum. One ball for each attacker. 4 bibs of one color, six of another. Four small goals. (Note, for clarity only, we have marked the balls as small grey circles.)

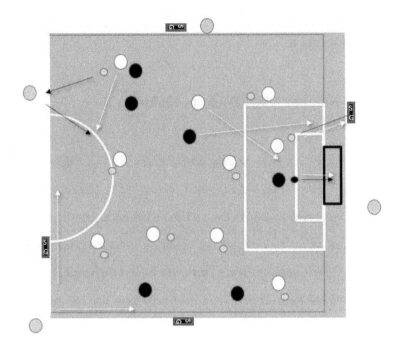

Method:

- *Twenty players in total.*
- *Ten attackers each have a ball in the grid.*
- *They must dribble to outside the grid to score one point.*
- *Six defenders can tackle any dribbler to prevent the score.*
- *If defenders win the ball, they dribble out of the grid anywhere and leave the ball for an attacker to collect. They score one point.*
- *Four 'pass target' players (grey players) wait outside the grid in order to receive a pass. These players cannot be*

tackled. When a dribbler feels they are likely to lose possession, they can make a safe pass to one of these targets and get a return pass when their defender has headed off elsewhere.

- *The 'pass targets' watch the game, move to where they are likely to be needed, and communicate their availability.*

Key Skills:

- *Dribble with head up.*
- *Accelerate away once player is beaten.*
- *Communication.*

Tip and Drill Number Eleven: Decision Making Rondo Game

This handy drill is helpful for encouraging players to keep moving once they have made the decision to pass or dribble.

Dribbling Aim: Dribble or pass to create a goal scoring opportunity.

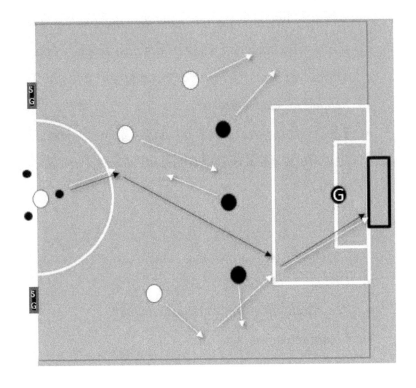

Equipment: Half pitch; goal at one end and two small goals at the other. Plentiful supply of balls.

Method:

- *Four attackers with no keeper v three defenders plus a keeper.*
- *Play starts with one attacker dribbling form the center circle.*
- *Attackers move to create space and lose their markers.*

- *Dribbler drives until pressured, then makes the best pass.*
- *Dribbler moves on into space for a return pass, or to draw a defender.*
- *Play continues until a shot on goal.*
- *If defenders win the ball they attempt to 'score' by passing the ball through either of the small goals at the other end.*

Key Skills:

- *Dribble with head up.*
- *Movement off the ball.*
- *Communication.*
- *Moving once a pass is made.*

Tip and Drill Number Twelve: Small Sided Game with Multiple Goals

A great drill for encouraging players to be patient in their build up play, allowing them time to make the right decision.

Dribbling Aim: To score a goal in any of five goals.

Equipment: Pitch with goals at either end, ball, four small goals made from cones.

Method:

- *6 v 6 or 7 v 7.*
- *Play a normal game.*
- *Goals are scored with a normal score for 3 points, or by dribbling through any of the small side goals for 1 point.*

Key Skills:

- *Players look for passes and dribbles sideways as well as forwards.*
- *Encourage players to use width to create space elsewhere on the pitch.*
- *Drive into the space when it is created forwards, creating a realistic game transition phase.*

Do not tolerate any criticism of a player who makes a decision, even if it turns out to be a wrong one. Such criticism must not be tolerated from teammates, or from parents and other supporters. Players improve by making mistakes. Short term wins are less important to a players' (and a team's!) development than the confidence to make decisions.

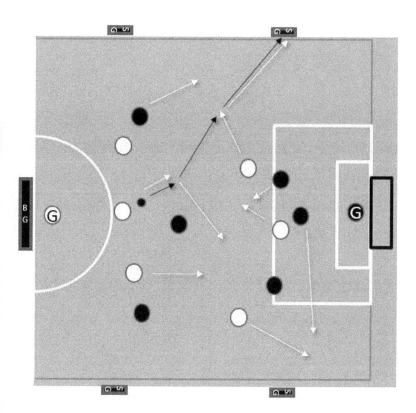

What is the biggest nightmare for a defender or central defensive midfielder? Probably, to be booked in the opening ten minutes of a game. The rest of the time that performer's ability to do their job of breaking down attacks is seriously compromised, because making one error in timing, or even (sadly, in the professional, and increasingly in the amateur game) an opponent 'winning' a foul, can get the player sent off.

Fortunately, such considerations are less important in the youth game, at least until the higher echelons are reached, since referees will rarely book players, and when a red card is given it will usually be for a single offence, rather than a combination.

That does not mean, however, that players should not consider their opponents in their decision making over whether to dribble or pass. It is a truism, if a rather crudish one, that a player that the dribbler expects to beat is the one to take on, and if that is not likely to happen, a pass is better. However, as we shall see, we can use drills and techniques to mitigate against the effective defender.

Tip and Drill Number Thirteen: Types of Player to Dribble Against

- *A player who shows poor technique when closing down; specifically, this will be a player who closes down chest on making it difficult for them to turn.*
- *A striker whose primary job when out of possession is to wait for the ball in transition, and who will therefore not wish to get involved in a lengthy chase back.*
- *A player who is slower than you.*
- *A player who is tall or has a high center of gravity making it difficult for them to turn.*
- *A player who is primarily one footed and can be dribbled at against their weaker foot.*
- *The last defender.*
- *Any defender when a teammate has made a good run which has distracted their attention.*

Tip and Drill Number Fourteen: Types of Player Who are Harder to Dribble Against

- *Players who do not like to commit themselves.*
- *Players who read the game well.*
- *Any player who, if they do tackle you, will be able to launch a devastating counterattack.*

Tip and Drill Number Fifteen: Trust Yourself! Stepover and Feint to Deliver a Pass

We will see drills and tips for skills to beat a defender in later chapters. However, the following drill is a good one for simply creating the space to make a pass, have a shot or deliver a cross.

As with much in soccer, the more two footed a player is*, the easier they will find this drill. The final aspect of it is still delivered under some pressure, and if the defender can work out which foot will play this final pass or shot, then it is easier for them to defend against it.

*(Later in the book we analyze whether two footedness really is the golden goal of soccer players, or an overblown myth).

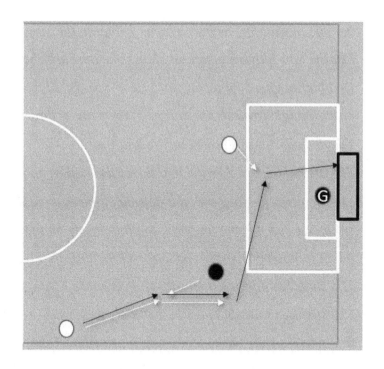

Dribbling Aim: Make the space to deliver an attacking threat.

Equipment: Half a junior pitch. Goal. Goalkeeper.

Method:

- *Six to eight players. Each run includes a dribbler, defender, support striker and goalkeeper. Players change roles after each run. For example, the dribbler moves next to support attacker, then defender, then joins the back of the line to wait for their next turn. (Note: in the diagram just the four players in action at any one time are shown.)*

- *Dribbler begins 30m from goal. He or she dribbles at a narrow angle towards the corner of the penalty box.*
- *The defender closes down, on the half turn.*
- *The dribbler steps over the ball with their weaker foot.*
- *This involves leading with the outside of the boot, and sweeping over the moving ball, to plant firmly on the side (right foot to right side of the ball, left to left).*
- *The shoulder dips towards the stepover foot.*
- *The stronger foot shifts the ball slightly to the side, right foot to right side, left to left, using the outside of the foot.*
- *Space is created as the defender follows the stepover foot, and in that time the dribbler shoots, passes or crosses to the support striker, whichever is the best option. (Note, the coach may need to instruct young defenders to 'buy' the stepover, since in this drill they know it is coming).*
- *For younger or less skilled players, it may be necessary to practice the stepover move unopposed until the player is comfortable with it.*

Key Skills (for the stepover):

- *Run with the ball with head up, on the toes controlling the ball with the laces.*
- *Move at the fastest pace that can be achieved whilst retaining control.*
- *Decide at the point of the step over whether it will be a shot, cross or pass. Any later and it will be difficult to maintain control.*
- *Use arms for balance when playing the ball.*

Basic Soccer Dribbling Drills to Create Space

Technically speaking, the purpose behind dribbling is to create space for oneself or a teammate. This works because dribbling draws the defense out of position. A defensive player must move out of their formation to close down the dribbler. This leaves a gap into which another player can work their magic.

The dribbler then has the opportunity to attempt to dribble past his opponent, causing even more mayhem, make the pass to a player who now has space or, if the situation is right, shift the ball for a shot or cross.

Tip and Drill Number Sixteen: Getting the First Touch Right

Nevertheless, the dribble will fail altogether if the receiver's first touch is not good. The following drill is simple to set up, fast paced and dynamic – all important characteristics of drills to use with youth footballers. As players get stronger, a second defender can be added whose sole role is to close down the outside receiver, thus putting pressure on his or her next pass.

Dribbling Aim: Improve first touch to create the opportunity to dribble.

Equipment: 20m x 20m grid. One ball.

Method:

- *Six players: One receiver who remains in the grid; four passers who each have one side of the grid; one defender who tries to win the ball off the receiver.*
- *Passer plays the ball in to the receiver's feet. The receiver controls the ball perfectly. If the control is good enough, turns and dribbles to another passer; if the control is less good, plays a pass back to the same passer.*
- *Receiver returns to the center of the grid.*
- *Passer now in possession either passes back to the receiver or passes across the grid to another team mate to change the angle of pass.*
- *Each successful dribble counts as one point, each pass 0 points but keep possession, each loss of possession each player changes until all have had a go in each position.*

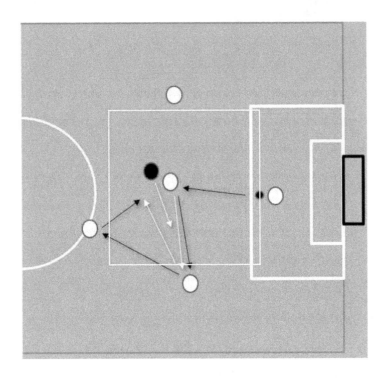

Key Skills (for controlling the ball):

- *Receive ball on the half turn.*
- *Ensure low center of gravity to allow for quick turn.*
- *Arms out for balance and to 'feel' the defender.*
- *First touch takes ball approx. ten to eighteen inches away from the body so the ball does not become stuck between feet.*

Tip and Drill Number Seventeen: Decision Making – Drawing the Defense

This is a handy drill, simple to operate and easy for even young players to pick up. The idea is that once the defender is beaten, another defender must move across, freeing up further space for support players.

The use of cones as defenders ensures that the key aims of the drill can be practised.

Dribbling Aim: Create space for a teammate by beating a defender.

Equipment: Three cones or mannequins, one ball. Half a junior pitch.

Method:

- *Four players; dribbler, support attacker, defender, keeper (optional).*
- *Three cones or mannequins; one approx. 10m outside the far corner of the penalty area ('marking' the support player). The second in line with the first, but midway between the opposite corner of the penalty area and the*

touchline. The final cone sits on the near side corner of the penalty area.

- *Dribbler runs at the cone, and dribbles past it.*
- *Dribbler must then pass into the support attacker before the line of the next cone is reached.*
- *The defender starts in the center of the penalty D and moves out towards the dribbler once he or she has 'beaten' the first cone. With very young or low skilled players, the drill can work without the physical defender.*
- *Meanwhile, once the defender moves, the support player moves off his cone (marker) and into the central space vacated by the defender.*
- *The support attacker receives the pass and attempts to score.*

Key Skills (for the dribbler):

- *Dribble at speed with head up.*
- *As the cone is approached, slow down slightly and get the ball under closer control.*
- *Try any skill to beat the cone.*
- *Cross low and into space.*
- *Judge the moment for the pass; not too soon to allow the physical defender to turn and challenge the support*

player, not too late when the angle for the pass can be cut out by the defender.

Tip and Drill Number Eighteen: Small Pitch Games (1) – Dribble to Death

Since the aim of this book is to improve players' dribbling skills and awareness, the more of this skill they can use, the better they will become at deploying it. This Rondo style drill is a good one for encouraging players to dribble, and keep the ball moving.

Dribbling Aim: To pass the ball once the dribble has created space.

Equipment: 20m x 20m grid (minimum – this drill needs plenty of space). One ball. No goals.

Method:

- *Six players in three groups of two.*
- *One pair are the defense, the other two pairs are the offensive players.*
- *Teams seek to keep possession for as long as possible. When possession is lost, or a rule breached, then the pair*

of the last offensive player to play the ball become the defense; the defense join the offense.

- *Passer dribbles until pressured and space created for others. Then they pass and move.*
- *Breaches which led to change of defense:*
  - o *Dribbler tackled.*
  - o *Pass intercepted.*
  - o *Ball dribbled/passed out of grid.*
  - o *Ball is stationary for more than two seconds.*
  - o *Three consecutive passes without a dribble. (Hence the attacking receiver can play an immediate pass, but this must be followed by a dribble, not another immediate pass. This is a dribbling drill!)*

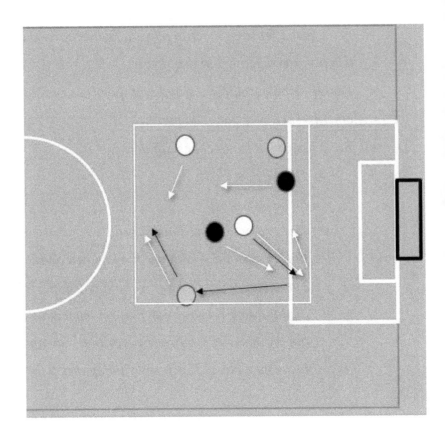

Key Skills (for utilizing space):

- *Receive ball on the half turn.*
- *Head swivel for options.*
- *Dribble with head up.*
- *Close control.*
- *Support players move to utilize space.*

Tip and Drill Number Nineteen: Small Pitch Games (2) Multiple goals

This is a handy drill for encouraging players to consider a variety of options to utilize space, rather than just a forward pass.

Dribbling Aim: Utilize space in all areas of the pitch. Dribble to create this space.

Equipment: Half pitch. One ball. Small 1-meter goals on all sides. One 1m grid in the middle of the pitch.

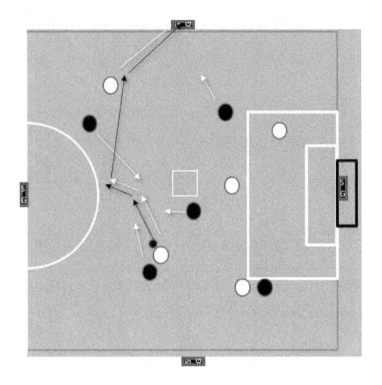

Method:

- *4 v 4 or 5 v 5. Play a normal game but coach encourages players to dribble to draw defenders and create space for teammates.*
- *Each time the ball is dribbled through a goal a point is scored. A point is also scored if the ball is dribbled through the central grid.*
- *After each 'score' the ball must be passed to an opponent.*

Key Skills:

- *Head up when dribbling.*
- *Movement and communication.*
- *Players must pass in whichever direction space exists.*

Tip and Drill Number Twenty: 6 v 4 Rondo Game to Create Space for the Dribble

Rondo games are excellent for developing skills, since some pressure exists but there is enough space to really practice the aim of the exercise.

This game is very similar to Drill 18, 'Dribble to Death'. However, it is played as a weighted match with small goals.

Dribbling Aim: Dribble to create space, then utilize this space.

Equipment: Half pitch. One ball. Two small goals one end, one small goal the other.

Method:

- *4 v 2; the larger team play into one goal; the smaller team have two in which they can score.*
- *Normal rules except no more than two passes are permitted by the larger team before they must dribble or shoot.*

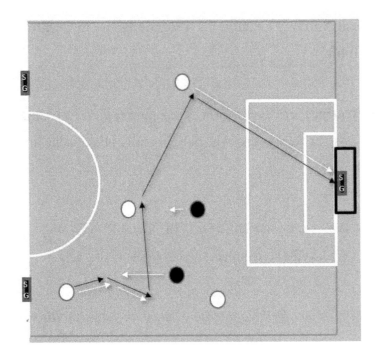

Key Skills (for controlling the ball):

- *Head up looking for space.*
- *Commit defenders then pass or beat player.*

- *Head swivel to check on space.*

Tip and Drill Number Twenty-One: 4 v 2 Turning into the Space Behind

Players will quickly learn that sometimes it is not possible to utilize the space created by a dribble, perhaps because the dribbler has become isolated, or there is no pass on, or the defense has doubled up.

In these scenarios, it is important to retain possession. The following drill is a good one to encourage players to check their options and be prepared to turn and start again. The coach explains to the player that when dribbling, space usually opens up directly behind the dribbler, like the way the wake of a ship splits the ocean behind it.

Dribbling Aim: Dribble, turn and pass.

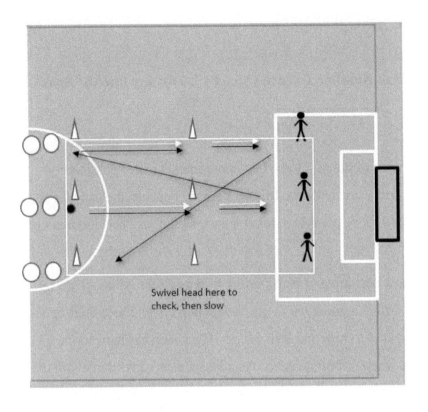

Swivel head here to
check, then slow

Equipment: 20m x 15m grid. Nine cones. One ball.

Method:

- Six players.
- Cones are spread as in the diagram above. Two players line up behind each of the three cones furthest from the goal. The middle cones mark the points players take a check over their shoulders to see what options are behind

them. The third cone in each line represents two defenders, necessitating a pass from the dribbler.

- *Dribbler runs at pace controlling the ball with their laces. At the middle cone, they check over their shoulder for their options.*

- *Players slow as they reach the 'defender' cone, then turn, and pass the ball back to any of the three first cones (each of which has one or two players ready to receive the pass).*

- *The drill is repeated by the player receiving the pass.*

- *After a few runs, change the positions of the players, as usually those on the central line will get most action.*

Key Skills (For checking):

- *Ensure players check both sides behind them.*

- *They may turn in any way they wish. As they become more skilled, they may develop more effective turning techniques, but that is not the principle aim of this drill.*

- *Ensure the pass is firm. Clearly, the drill creates an artificial situation, with no active defensive players, but young soccer players sometimes need to be reminded that we practice drills as close to match situations as we can.*

Tip and Drill Number Twenty-Two: Running off the Dribbler to Create Space (1)

The final drill in this section focusses on the support player rather than the dribbler. The support player's runs not only create space for the pass but can also create space for the dribbler. The following drill can help young players to understand the importance of running off the ball, and once in place can be translated to match practices.

Dribbling Aim: Run off the ball to create space for the dribbler.

Equipment: Half pitch. One ball.

Method:

- *Two attackers, one defender and a goalkeeper.*
- *Dribbler runs at defender.*
- *Support player makes a run; shouting for the pass (it is important that the defense is aware of the support player's run!)*
- *If defense player moves towards the run, dribbler takes them on and tries to get in a shot.*

- *If defense does not track the runner, or create space for the dribbler, then a pass is made, and the support player attempts to score.*

- *Coach focusses on praise for the support runner, since making runs can be a thankless task. This praise must be translated into the match situation.*

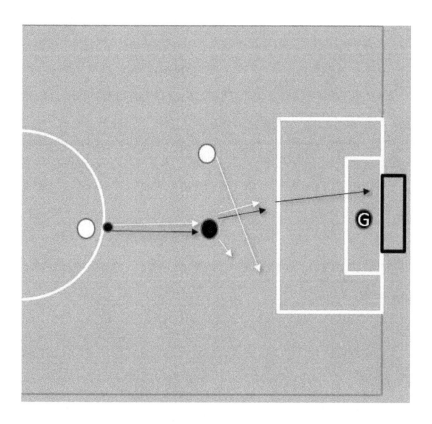

Key Skills (for support player):

- *Run into space.*

- *Move across the defender, to draw their attention and set them a problem.*

- *Communicate the run to attract the defense's attention.*

- *Expect the pass, don't be disappointed if it does not come.*

Tip and Drill Number Twenty-Three: 'Head on the Swivel'

The term really means that a player must be aware of what is going on around them. In other words, whilst their concentration will be on the ball, they must sense – look, listen and develop periphery vision – for movement of teammates.

Encourage players to look at top players receiving the ball and see how they assess their options whilst waiting for the ball to reach them. Suggest they watch clips of great dribblers from the modern game to see how they keep their heads up and checking to see what passes might be on.

The next stage, of course, is assessing the 'best' option a dribbler can take; this decision cannot be reached if the player is unaware of all their available choices.

The Dribble Leading to an Assist

In the previous chapter we focused very much on the importance of seeing dribbling as a whole pitch exercise which can deliver benefit in creating space anywhere on the park.

However, we do not wish to detract in any way from the offensive values of dribbling. In this chapter we look at drills in which dribbling leads to the possibility of an assist.

Tip and Drill Number Twenty-Four: Dribbling for the By-line Cross

It is true that the game has moved on; maybe the ideas of a winger driving to the by line, putting over a cross and the striker rising high to head home is a little old fashioned. Nevertheless, it remains an important part of the game, possibly even more so at amateur levels than in the professional game.

Perhaps the one area of soccer where the skill is least employed is in the youth game. The US has for a while now banned heading for the very youngest age groups. Other countries across the soccer playing world are beginning to follow suit. Even in the nation that created the game – Britain – heading for younger players is soon to be banned – although in typically half-hearted fashion the English FA has decided to ban heading in training for Under Elevens and below, but not in match situations. There are plenty of coaches and commentators (not to mention parents) who feel that this move is akin to sending a soldier to the front line but neglecting to give him any training with regards to what he might expect there.

Still, this is a coaching book, not one to delve into the bizarre decision making of the world's various football (soccer) associations. However, with this drill we have included the use of mannequins (ideally) or cones rather than defenders in the penalty area, and are suggesting that the drill is used as a secondary double goalkeeping session, with the second keeper catching the high cross, and hitting a low one first time (also a useful skill) rather than heading the ball.

Clearly, where coaches are working with older youth groups, and are confident that heading is safe for them, the cones and second keeper can be replaced with strikers and defense. Notwithstanding this, we strongly urge coaches to consider the safety factors involved in heading the ball. Scientists are learning all of the time about the risks of concussion and early onset dementia which may be linked to heading the ball.

Dribbling Aim: Dribble to the byline and cross.

Equipment: Half pitch. Several balls. Mannequins or, failing this, cones.

Method:

- *One dribbler, one defender, one 'normal' keeper, one second keeper replacing forward for high crosses, acting as a forward for low ones.*

- *One cone is set on the corner of the box. There is a mannequin to cut out the cross at the near post; a second can be used centrally with stronger players.*

- *The second keeper starts deep on the far post, ready to run in to either catch a cross away from the main keeper or hit a first time shot for a low cross.*

- ***Safety Note: Warn keepers of the danger of clashing. With younger players it may be wise to set limits on where each keeper can operate.***

- *Dribbler runs at pace down the wing. When level with the defender, this player attempts to close down the cross.*

- *Winger dribble to byline and whips in cross, low or high.*

- *Once move completed, the winger becomes the defender and the defender joins the back of the line ready for another turn. The next player sets off.*

Key Skills (for support player):

- *Use arms for balance.*
- *Look up to see position of defense and teammates.*
- *Plant the non-kicking foot next to the ball.*
- *Ensure the hips are at an angle to the ball.*
- *Strike the ball firmly but smoothly.*

Tip and Drill Number Twenty-Five: Dribble for the Pull Back

This drill works in exactly the same was as Drill Twenty-Four above. However, because the ball will be pulled back low, there is no heading risk. Use cones to represent defenders, but once players become more competent, replace the cones with actual defenders.

The cut back is a very effective tool. When a player dribbles towards the by line, the defense will move back with him or her. This can often leave a gap between the penalty spot and edge of the area into which a player can pull for the shot or arrive late for the shot.

Dribbling Aim: Dribble and Pull Back to Create a Scoring Chance.

Equipment: Half pitch. One ball. Cones or real defenders.

Method:

- *Dribbler, two attackers and one keeper. (Up to three defenders if using these).*
- *Dribbler runs at pace towards the by line.*
- *Advanced support player angles run, changes direction and heads towards the near post.*
- *Support player two arrives late to the edge of the box.*

- *Dribbler pulls the ball back low towards the penalty spot/edge of area.*
- *Teammates attempt to score.*
- *Change the roles regularly.*

Key Skills (for dribbler):

- *Look up before crossing.*
- *Pull the ball back and away from the keeper.*
- *Aim to hit the area into which players are running, rather than the player themselves; they stand the best chance of scoring if they are running onto the ball.*

Tip and Drill Number Twenty-Six: Dribbling on the Wrong Side – Cutting Back onto the Stronger Foot and Cross

This drill uses many of the techniques of the drill above. However, the winger is on their 'weaker foot' so they cut back and play a lateral pass rather than a pull back. Again, a cone can be used instead of a defender.

Tip and Drill Number Twenty-Seven: Crossing from either side

A clever game in which teams attempt to get the ball wide to a dribbler who runs into the crossing zone and delivers a ball. Goals can only be scored with assists from wide crosses, and crosses can only be made after dribbling.

Only one defender is allowed in each wide area (marked by cones or grids) and no defense is permitted in the red zones, from where crosses can be made. (Just the attacking half is shown on the diagram below).

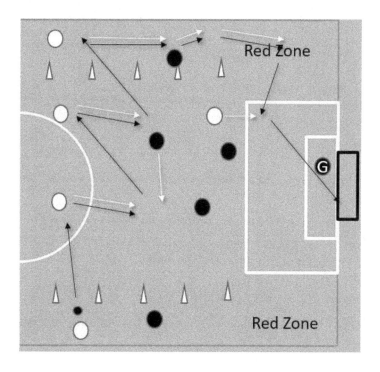

Dribbling Aim: Practise crossing assists.

Equipment: Pitch, cones/lines marking out wide areas and red zones.

Method:

- *Two teams, normal game with restrictions.*
- *Goals can only be scored following assists from the wide areas or red zones.*
- *Attackers cannot pass into the red zone; the ball must be dribbled into it.*
- *No defense in the red zone (but attempts to stop crosses can still be made), only one defender in the wide areas.*

Key Skills (for team):

- *Work the ball into the wide areas.*
- *Make good runs into the box to score from crosses and pull backs.*
- *Deliver quality crosses.*

Tip and Drill Number Twenty-Eight: Dribble Centrally to create an assist

A driven dribble through the middle can be just as effective at creating an assist. This 3 v 2 drill requires a defender to be drawn out of position allowing the dribbler to play in a pass towards the space vacated.

Dribbling Aim: Dribble to create space, time and weight the pass to score.

Equipment: Half pitch. One ball.

Method:

- *Dribbler, two support attackers, two defenders and a goalkeeper.*
- *Dribbler starts at center spot and drives towards the defense.*
- *Support players advance from either side.*
- *Two defenders begin on the edge of their box and close down space.*
- *Dribbler commits a defender, then slips through a pass for a teammate (if the defense fails to close down the dribbler, she can simply shoot).*
- *Change roles after each turn.*

Key Skills (for dribbler):

- *Drive forward at pace, head up and propelling the ball with the laces.*
- *Slow as defender approaches and bring the ball under tighter control.*
- *Head swivel to pick out support strikers' runs.*
- *Shift the ball slightly and weight the pass into space.*

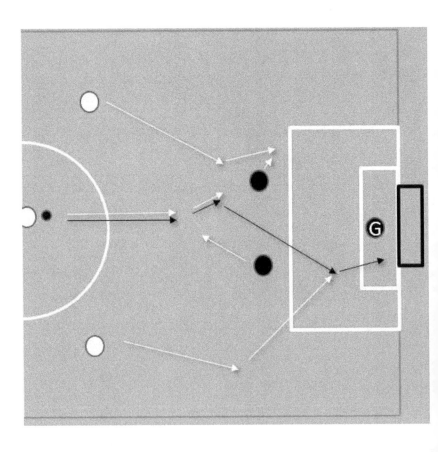

INDIVIDUAL SKILLS OF A DRIBBLER

The Fake: Feinting and Turning the Other Way

We have focused so far very much on dribbling as a part of team play. We have looked at how a strong dribble can create space for teammates, and the dribbler themselves. We have examined crossing, passing for a striker to run on, dribbling laterally as well as forwards and the importance of using the space behind the dribbler.

In this the second half of the book we will look in detail at the actual skills of the dribbler. The techniques which allows him to beat a player or gives her the space to deliver a killer pass, or fire off a devastating shot.

We'll start this section with a look at one of the key skills any dribbler will need. A feint is a move which will by a fraction of a second of time; enough to go part an opponent, make a key pass or cross, and fire off a shot.

Tip and Drill Number Twenty-Nine: Dropping the Shoulder

Enacted at pace, there is almost no defense against a shoulder drop. The dribbler drops a shoulder and plants the foot on the same side to suggest that they are heading in one direction, then sweeps the ball with the outside of the opposite foot in the opposite direction to the shoulder.

The planted foot then comes into play, with the player driving off this to accelerate away.

Young children can take a while to acquire the skill, so a simple cone drill both helps to develop the basis skill set needed for the feint. It can also help to remove the tendency to only drop the shoulder on one side (which a clever defender will soon work out.

This drill is aimed very much at beginners, and because the skills needed are not natural ones, we have eliminated the ball, which can be added later. This allows young player to concentrate on movements alone.

Dribbling Aim: Drop the shoulder to create space with a feint.

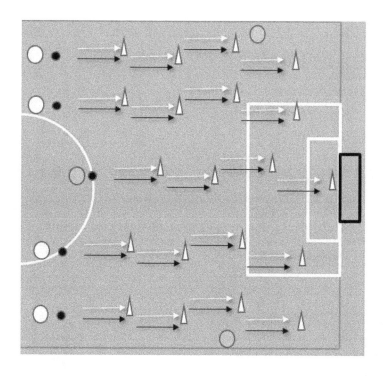

Equipment: Large area – half pitch minimum. Several lines of cones.

Method:

- *The coach or an older player leads, with a second helper watching the children and intervening where they go wrong.*
- *The remaining players follow behind, copying the moves.*
- *Pace can increase as the children become more competent.*

- *Approach the first cone, drop left shoulder, plant left foot, simulate moving ball with outside of right foot, push off left foot and accelerate away. (If the right foot has planted, following the dummy movement, push off this).*
- *The sweep of the ball goes in the opposite direction to the shoulder drop, shifting the ball approximately half a meter past the imaginary off balance defender.*
- *At the next cone repeat the move using the right foot and shoulder.*

Key Skills (for dribbler):

- *Exaggerate the shoulder drop.*
- *Keep low to increase drive off the planted foot.*
- *When a ball is introduced, do not shift it too far. It should be possible for the kicking foot to catch up and straighten the line of the ball in no more than one step. Even better is to straighten the ball before the kicking foot hits the ground.*

Tip and Drill Number Thirty: Stand Still and Feint

Sometimes a dribbler can break away from teammates. In this case, if there is a reasonably organized defense in front, it can be useful to slow down the break to await support. This slowing down also provides a good opportunity to feint past an opponent.

Dribbling Aim: Feint from a standing position.

Equipment: Half pitch, several cones, enough balls for one each.

Method:

- *Set up the pitch as for the drill above.*
- *Player dribbles to a cone, stops, feints from a standing position and moves on to the next cone.*
- *Feint is achieved by dropping the shoulder on one side then another, while faking the shift of the ball with the outside of each foot.*
- *The dribbler makes the decision when to actually complete the feint, then accelerates away in the same manner as in the drill above.*

Key Skills (for dribbler):

- *Exaggerate movements.*
- *Rotate the arms to add to the confusion for the defender.*

- *In a match situation, the decision as to when to complete the feint will be determined by:*
  - *A defender committing themselves to making the tackle.*
  - *The arrival of support.*

Tip and Drill Number Thirty-One: Cross and Feint

This useful trick can be employed to create space at the start of a dribble. It is a risky maneuver and is best tried either when losing the ball is not catastrophic or when there is little risk of losing the ball. For example, when a ball is played across the back four, and an attacker is closing to apply pressure, but is not close enough to win the ball. It is a trick often used by goalkeepers receiving a back pass.

Dribbling Aim: Allow the ball to cross the body, before accelerating in the opposite way to begin a dribble.

Equipment: Large area, at least 25 m x 25 m. Balls, mannequins of cones.

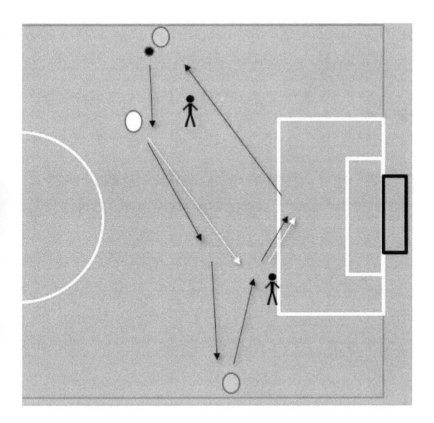

Method:

- *Two feeders, line of receivers to practice the feint.*
- *The ball is fed in from the side by the coach.*
- *Player moves towards the pass slightly, half turned, as though to control it with the outside of the leading foot.*
- *The player drops their body position and dummies the ball to let it run across their body.*

- *Player edges the ball forward with the instep of their other foot, changing the angle by 30-45 degrees.*
- *Player accelerates away with the ball.*
- *For the drill, player dribbles 10 meters then passes to another feeder who returns the pass.*
- *Dribbler then repeats the feint past a second mannequin going in the opposite direction before dribbling on, then back to the rear of the line waiting their turn.*

Key Skills (for dribbler):

- *Rapid change of direction at the dummy point.*
- *Let the ball roll across the front of the body, do not reach for it with the furthest foot.*
- *Drive hard into the space created.*

Tip and Drill Number Thirty-Two: Dummy Air Shot

Again, a risky move because if a defender does not buy the feint, the dribbler is off balance for a short time and likely to be tackled. However, the natural reaction for a player trying to face another at close range is to back their head and body away from what they think is a shot or firmly hit, lifted pass.

That movement gives the dribbler a moment to knock the ball past the stricken defender before they can recover.

The drill below is popular with young players because they enjoy the drama of a 'fake' shot, and also the involvement that comes in very small sided games.

Dribbling Aim: Fake a shot (or lofted pass if deeper on the pitch) to fool the defense. Use the space created to move the ball past the defender.

Equipment: 20 m x 10 m grid. Lots of balls. Cones for small goals at either end

Method:

- *2 v 2 (this game also works with a 1 v 1). Make a small goal, 1 meter wide, at either end.*
- *Goals are scored by dribbling or shooting through the cones.*
- *Players make the dummy air shot, and use the space created to dribble, pass or shoot.*

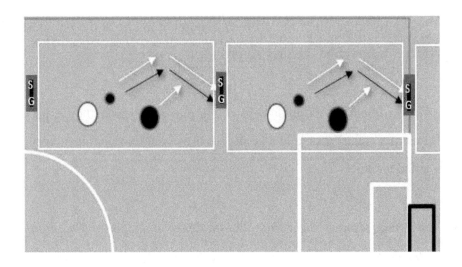

Key Skills (for dribbler):

- *Exaggerate the air shot.*
- *Usually it is best to use the shooting foot (instep or outside or the boot) to move the ball either way past the defender.*
- *The dribbler should select the direction opposite to where the player has committed. This is not essential, as there is often a lot of time created if the opponent buys the air shot.*
- *Use the entire body, arms, voice, head, in making the feint shot.*

Tip: This is very useful if the defender has fully committed to stopping the shot. If not, it may be better to go for the shot.

Tip and Drill Number Thirty-Three: Using the Eyes

The eyes *are essential in these feinting drills. Every part of the body is key in creating a false impression of where the dribbler intends to move, but the eyes are more effective than any other at deceiving an opponent. Good defenders will try to look only at the ball, but rapid movements are likely to encourage them to look up, and it is then that a dummy with the eyes (looking in the opposite direction to that which the dribbler intends to move) or even a double bluff, can be conclusive.*

The Quick Step Over and Turn

The modern master of the step over is undoubtedly Cristiano Ronaldo. Watching the former Manchester United, Real Madrid and current Juventus forward in full flow is truly a joy, and an excellent exemplar for any young player seeking to learn the skills of dribbling.

Ronaldo makes the skill look easy and, to be fair, it is not the hardest soccer technique to learn. However, the great striker's particular ability is to perform the step over at speed, and on multiple occasions when beating his defender.

However, we can break the step over down into its constituent parts:

Tip and Drill Number Thirty-Four: Technical Aspects of the Step Over

- *The ball must remain in playing distance of the feet; Ronaldo keeps the ball about half a meter or less in front of him until the point his glides past his full back.*
- *The foot moves quickly over the ball, close to it but without touching. The double step over sees the other foot repeat the move in the opposite direction.*
- *The dribblers body should be:*
  - *Slightly bent at the waist.*
  - *Arms used for balance.*
  - *Head up.*

Tip and Drill Number Thirty-Five: Basic Introduction

Even young players can pick up the step over quickly. The following very basic drill allows them to practice. The coach circulates checking technique.

Dribbling Aim: Master the technique of the step over.

Equipment: Several balls. Cones.

Method:

- *Players work in groups of three. A 10-meter strip is marked out with a cone at each end. Two players begin at one end with a ball, the other player waits by the other cone.*
- *The first player dribbles slowly, completing a step over in the middle.*
- *The ball is dribbled on to the teammate who repeats the exercise.*
- *Once the basic technique is mastered introduce the double step over.*
- *Practice at increasing speed.*

Key Skills (for dribbler):

- *Follow the analysis of Ronaldo above.*

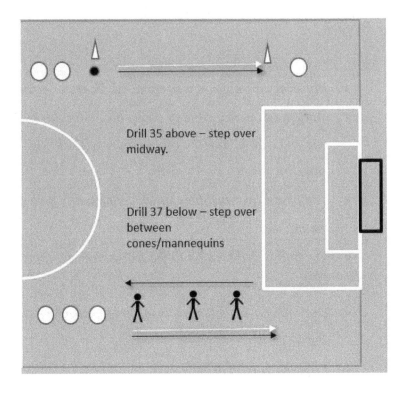

Drill 35 above – step over midway.

Drill 37 below – step over between cones/mannequins

Tip and Drill Number Thirty-Six: Tip Regarding Coaching the Step Over to Young Players

It can be tempting to get each child to practice individually, as the coach watches. However, youngsters need action and movement, and will become bored and disruptive if they are waiting for long periods for their 'turn'.

Tip and Drill Number Thirty-Seven: Advanced Step Over

This drill repeats drill thirty-five above but includes
cones/mannequins to dribble round. These should be approximately 5
meters apart. Make the course long and have several players using it at
the same time. Once the course is completed, players run at pace with
their ball back to their place in the line.

Dribbling Aim: Master the Step Over.

*Equipment: 30 m x 10 m grid. Lots of balls. Cones to represent
defenders.*

Method:

- *Dribble at pace and use a step over to beat each cone
  defender.*
- *Alternate the direction of step over at each cone.*

Key Skills (for dribbler):

- *As above.*

Tip and Drill Number Thirty-Eight: Step over and Shoot

This drill is for more advanced players. With younger players, use a mannequin or cone as a defender rather than a real player. The use of wide players adds pressure on the defender, making the step over a little easier as the attacker has more time on the ball.

Dribbling Aim: Utilize the step over to create a shooting opportunity.

Equipment: Half pitch. Several balls. Three cones to mark starting points.

Method:

- *Three attackers, one pivot, two defenders, goalkeeper.*
- *The pivot calls for a pass from any of the three strikers waiting by their cones.*
- *A defender closes on the pivot, who lays off a pass to any of the three strikers, who are now advancing.*
- *The player receiving the pass now dribbles hard towards the goal. The other attackers become support players.*

- *The dribbler attempts a step over to create space for a shot. If this is not on, then a pass is made to another forward who also shoots.*

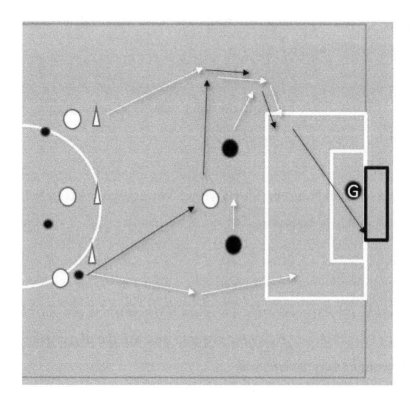

Key Skills:

- *Create shooting opportunities for both feet, not just the stronger one.*
- *Support players and spare defender chase in rebounds.*

The Dribble and Complete Turn

There are times in soccer when a player may need to undertake a complete turn in control of the ball. For example, when he or she has broken away from team mates and needs to wait for support, or when the player is confronted by a wall of defense and needs to turn back towards their own team.

In this chapter we will consider ways to improve turning with the ball.

Tip and Drill Number Thirty-Nine: Young Players Can Self Analyze Their Decisions

A handy coaching tip is to stop games when a player becomes isolated, attempts a dribble and, even if successful at the outset, the move breaks down. ***Reset the position and ask the player what options they might have considered.***

Tip and Drill Number Forty: Turning with the Right Foot

This is a simple drill which is handy to use in a warm up.

Dribbling Aim: Keep close control with one foot, while turning.

Equipment: Penalty area or similar size. One ball each.

Method:

- *Each player has a ball. They must dribble around the area without bumping into teammates or losing control of the ball.*
- *They can use their stronger foot only.*
- *The drill can be repeated for use with the weaker foot (!)*

Key Skills (for dribbler):

- *Head up.*
- *Keep the ball within half a meter of the foot, under close control.*
- *Use both the inside and outside of the foot to change direction.*

Tip and Drill Number Forty-One: Assault Course

A fun drill which involves players showing dexterity with the ball. Children love the challenge element of the drill.

Dribbling Aim: Move in various directions with the ball under close control.

Equipment: 30 m x 10 m grid. Lots of balls. Mannequins and cones for obstacles. Example below.

Method:

- *Set up series of obstacles; flags in poles, pairs of cones, sets of cones to dribble through etc.*
- *Order the obstacles so the dribbler must follow a set path.*

- *Time each run. Quickest wins. Put a 30 second penalty whenever the player loses control through an obstacle or misses one.*
- *Start the next runner as soon as the previous one has completed a third of the course.*

Key Skills (for dribbler):

- *Head up.*
- *Focus on completing the task, rather than what is going on around them. (Often those waiting get excited and noisy as their peers attempt the course).*
- *Keep the ball under close control.*
- *Use both feet, instep and outside.*

Tip and Drill Number Forty-Two: Turn with the Outside of the Foot

When the ball is played into feet to a player with their back to goal, they face a choice. Either lay the ball off to a teammate or turn and run at the opposing defense. This drill can be adapted to various levels of pressure from the defense.

Dribbling Aim: Control a ball to feet and make a wide turn.

Equipment: Large area so that several groups can work at once.

Method:

- *Feeder, receiver and defender.*
- *The feeder lays in a 10-meter pass to feet. The feeder then moves off to make an angle for a return pass (a good habit for the match situation).*
- *Receiver moves to the half turn and extends front foot to take the ball on the outside of the foot.*
- *Keeping low, and with the ball under control. The receiver turns in a wide arc using the outside of their foot until they are facing their opponent's goal.*
- *Defender puts controlled pressure to allow the drill to work.*
- *Change roles*

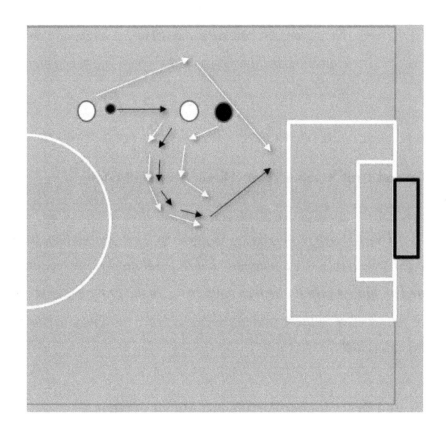

Key Skills (on receiving the ball):

- *Body low to facilitate turn.*
- *Arms out and feeling for defender.*
- *Chest at 45 degrees to the ball.*
- *Depending of the pressure from the defense, turn the front foot to direct the ball on the first stage of the turning arc.*

- *The tighter the pressure, the wider the angle of turn to enable the dribbler to keep their body between defender and ball.*

Tip and Drill Number Forty-Three: Decision Making

*The best soccer players make good decisions more often. In order to assist with this, use a **magnetic board to set up various scenarios of the ball played into the striker**. Discuss with the group the best options for the receiver in these situations. Should they turn, and dribble? Or pass and run?*

Tip and Drill Number Forty-Four: Match situation

Play an artificial match whereby at every restart player move to a set position which allows the ball to be played in two feet for a striker to attempt a turn. Permit a lay off as well, so the striker must decide on the best option in the circumstances.

Changing Direction While Dribbling

The ability to change direction whilst dribbling is crucial to maintaining possession. This might be to buy time while support arrives, to change the angle for a pass, or to prepare for a shot.

Changing direction can create space for teammates, especially an overlap when cutting in from the wing. There are various skills and techniques to achieve this ability to change direction while dribbling, some of which we will cover in this chapter.

Tip and Drill Number Forty-Five: The Inside Turn

This turn buys some time and space when a defender is shadowing the dribbler. It is a useful weapon in a player's arsenal. If a defense is aware that a player is adept at using the inside turn, they may give the space for an effective feint as they prepare for the turn.

Dribbling Aim: Execute the Inside Turn

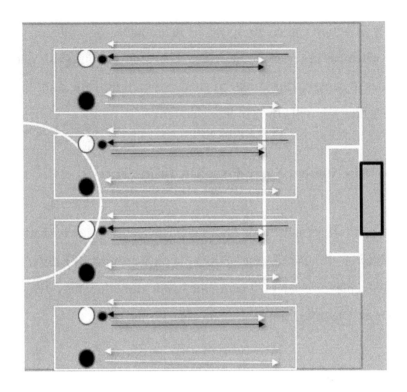

Equipment: Narrow corridor 20 m x 5 m. Ball.

Method:

- *Dribbler v defender.*
- *Dribble down channel while defender shadows.*
- *Complete the inside turn.*
    - *Dribbler keeps their body between the ball and the defender.*

- The outside foot stretches beyond the ball and plays the ball back in the opposite direction to travel.
- The instep is used to bring the ball back.
- Make sure that the body is between the ball and the defender when you make the turn.
- Dribble back along the channel and repeat the turn.
- After four turns swap roles.

Key Skills (for dribbler):

- *Body between ball and defender.*
- *Swivel hips on turn.*
- *Accelerate on changing direction to create some space.*

Tip and Drill Number Forty-Six: Changing Direction

Show the defense your versatility by demonstrating various skills, including the inside turn, early in the game. This will create doubt in the opposition's mind.

Tip and Drill Number Forty-Seven: Changing Direction Under Close Control

Faced with a 1 v 1 situation, the dribbler will often use a change of pace as a key part of beating their opponent. Combining this with a rapid change of direction is an effective partnership indeed. The following drill is intense and helps with fitness as well as skills.

Dribbling Aim: Change Direction and Dribble Away.

Equipment: Four cones marking a 10 m square. One ball each.

Method:

- *Lay out the square. The player dribbles around the square five times, then repeats using their other foot.*
- *On the first side of the square advance with short steps, propelling the ball with the outside of the foot.*
- *At the first corner, dip the shoulder, accelerate and push the ball at 90 degrees around the square.*
- *Push the ball further ahead along this side, now with the laces, to simulate accelerating away from an opponent.*
- *At the second corner, turn and repeat the first side with short movements.*

- *On the final side sprint once more.*
- *Then swap to repeat the exercise with the other foot.*

Key Skills (for dribbler):

- *Head up.*
- *Short steps on the toes, running at half speed on the slow side.*
- *Drop the shoulder and drive on the turn*
- *Move the ball always with the outside of the foot on the short side, with the laces on the acceleration sides, but always under control.*

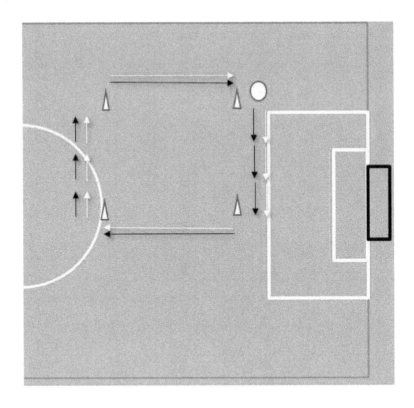

Tip and Drill Number Forty-Eight: The Outside Hook

This move is similar to the inside cut, but whilst that move is often used as a precursor to laying the ball back, or dribbling for a better position, the outside hook is a more aggressive move, and is especially effective when a player is dribbling on the 'wrong side', that is, for example, a right footed player on the left side.

This advantage comes from the fact that the turn is later than with the inside cut, and therefore the defender is more likely to continue past the turn, leaving some space.

Dribbling Aim: Perfect the Outside Hook.

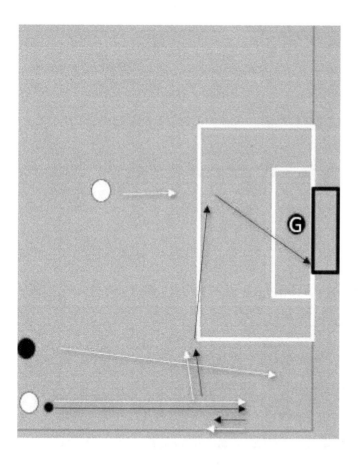

Equipment: Quarter pitch, wide, with goal at one end. One ball per group.

Method:

- *Dribbler, shooter, defender and goalkeeper.*
- *The dribbler dribbles wide, with the defender shadowing.*
- *Dribbler places outside foot between defender and ball.*
- *Dribbler hooks the ball back 180 degrees using the outside of the foot.*
- *Dribbler swivels hips, drives off planted foot, drops body position and sprints onto the ball.*
- *While defender recovers, dribbler either crosses first time, or dribbles on and passes.*
- *Shooter attempts to score.*
- *Change roles and repeat.*
- *Work on both feet.*

Key Skills (for dribbler):

- *Change of pace on turn.*
- *Drive into the space created.*
- *Look up before passing.*
- *Utilize the space – do not give the defender a chance to recover.*

Dribbling with the Inside and Outside of the Foot

Developing dexterity with both the inside and outside of both feet is important for the skill of dribbling. A player who is solely one footed is much easier to defend against than one comfortably using both. The options a one footed player has to beat an opponent are less than a two footed player can offer.

Equally, players must be comfortable dribbling with both parts of the foot (we will come on to running with the ball using the laces in a later chapter). A player who is only adept with their inside will struggle to dribble at pace, whilst a player who can only use the outside of their foot will be limited in their direction changing and lateral movements.

Tip and Drill Number Forty-Nine: Using Instep and Outside of the Foot - Basic

With young children, the following drill is handy. Have plenty of dribble tracks on the go at once to keep the young players active.

Dribbling Aim: Change Direction and Dribble Away.

Equipment: Several tracks of six cones, each approximately two meters apart. One ball per track.

Method:

- *Players dribble through the cones using the outside and instep of their feet.*
- *On reaching the final cone, they pass the ball back to the next player then jog to the end of the line.*
- *Focus on technique at the outset, then build up speed as confidence and competence grow.*

Key Skills (for dribbler):

- *Head up.*
- *Face the direction of travel, i.e., straight down the line of the cones.*
- *It is fine to use one foot for the drill, instep and outside, provided both feet are used.*
- *Keep the body low, with arms out for balance.*
- *The ball should always be close to the body, within playing distance (no more than half a meter from the foot.)*

- *Aim for two touches to go through each cone; one to slow the ball, the other to move it. As the player advances reduce this to one touch.*

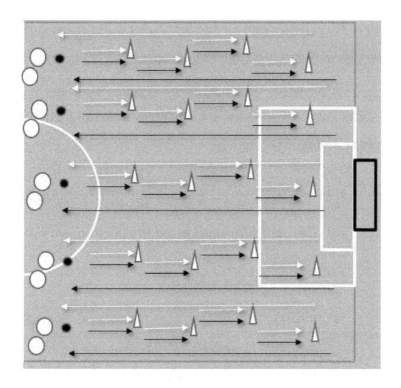

Tip and Drill Number Fifty: Keep It Active

*When using drills with lines of cones, ensure that players are not standing still for too long. Young players have **very limited concentration spans**.*

Tip and Drill Number Fifty-One: Coaching Large Groups

A problem a coach can face when running any drill where many players are active (which, of course, we always want) is dealing with players who are making technical mistakes. The best way of addressing this is to have assistants who can help – this could be older youth players as well as adult coaches.

*However, this problem can be alleviated in two ways **peer coaching and positioning**:*

- *Peer coaching: Divide the players into small groups of varying ability and get the players to coach each other. Youngsters love doing this.*

- *Position yourself, as coach, as follows. Imagine a giant rectangle is covering the entire area in which the drill is taking place. The coach stands at one corner of the rectangle, opposite where the waiting players are lined up. This means that all students are within eyesight at all times, and the players in action are closer to the coach than those waiting. See the diagram below, which relates to the previous drill, number 49.*

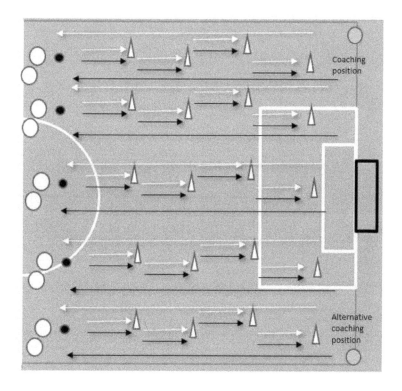

Coaching position

Alternative coaching position

Tip and Drill Number Fifty-Two: Embedding the Skill

There are only so many cone tracks drill that players will enjoy doing, and therefore other methods can be useful to embed the skills. An effective way is to put controls on other drills and match practices which are short – no more than a minute; usually thirty seconds is enough – to concrete the skill in players.

For example:

- *In a match practice, say all dribbles must use both parts of the foot or a free kick is given.*
- *During a running warm up with the ball, instruct use of the instep and outside of the foot.*
- *Stop any other drill and get players to practice dribbling for thirty seconds using both parts of both feet.*

Tip and Drill Number Fifty-Three: Priorities in Coaching

For any drill, with young players, it is better to keep players active and working, and risk missing a technical fault than to have only one student or small group active at a particular moment.

However, once good discipline is established in the group, and the coach is confident that the majority will get on with the task in hand, it is strong practice to spend a short but intensive period with a small group or individual.

*It is worth **keeping a record of this intense 1 to 1 or small group coaching**. It is easy for a coach to inadvertently, over a period, spend a disproportionate time on particular players – often the best or the most in need of coaching. This can cause resentment among other players (often reinforced by parents!) even though the additional attention might be deserved or unintended.*

Running with The Ball vs Dribbling

Running with the ball and dribbling are close siblings, maybe even twins, but not identical ones. By implication, dribbling involves running at an opponent with the intention of creating space by drawing a defender to you. Dribbling will often result with taking a player on, looking to beat them with pace and skill. Dribbling will occur using a variety of techniques, tricks and changes in acceleration.

By contrast running with the ball is what takes place when a player has space in front of them. Effective running with the ball involves moving at top speed in a straight line to cover the ground as quickly as possible. As every time the ball is touched the player must slow fractionally (or more, for weaker players) as they adjust their feet to control and propel the ball, running with the ball involves knocking it further in front of feet than when dribbling, so fewer touches are needed. However, the ball is still kept under control so a defender cannot move across and intercept.

Often, running with the ball will turn into a dribble as the defense closes. At that point, players may slow a little, gain closer control of the ball, use the outside of the foot (on the little toe) to propel it rather than the laces which are used when traveling at full speed.

Tip and Drill Number Fifty-Five: Identifying When to Run with the Ball

This is to do with space. **Create scenarios on the pitch, or using a magnetic board, and discuss with players what the person in possession should do.** *Dribble run with the ball or pass.*

The answer will depend on the space, the support available and the state of the defense. *Driving at the defense can be the best option when there is* **space** *and* **any advanced players are isolated** *against a defense which outnumbers them.* *Spend no more than five minutes on this kind of tactical drill, as attention will quickly fade.*

Tip and Drill Number Fifty-Five: Running with the Ball Technique – Using the Laces

This is an easy to operate drill, with plenty of action for players. The size of the grid depends on the ages of the players. The drill also helps players to practice a pass at the end of the run, teaching them to weight the pass carefully as their momentum can often result in an overhit pass.

Dribbling Aim: Run with the ball using laces

Equipment: 30 m x 10m grid, with the narrow side divided into two channels. One ball per grid.

Method:

- *Minimum three players, but several channels can be used at once. The opposite side of the grid can also be used with more advanced players. They will need to time their pass carefully in this situation.*
- *Two players at one end, one (or two) at the other in the opposite channel.*
- *Run with the ball at speed, using the laces to avoid breaking stride and pushing the ball approximately five meters ahead in a straight line.*
- *Ten meters from the end, make a diagonal pass into the adjacent channel for the next player to run back. Move into the opposite channel to wait for the next turn.*
- *By changing the channel that is used to begin the run, the direction of the final pass is also changed.*

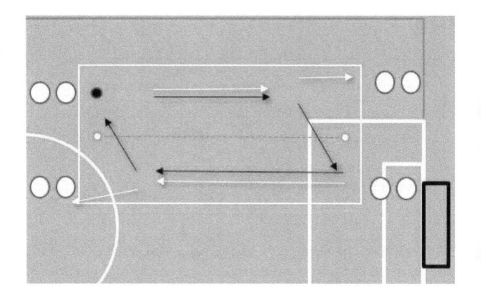

Key Skills (for runner):

- *Head up.*
- *Run as fast as possible, on toes.*
- *Time strides so that the ball is propelled without breaking step.*
- *Push the ball forwards about five meters with the laces. Players should reach the ball just as it is slowing down.*
- *Concentrate on the final diagonal pass, learning to weight the pass depending on running speed. There is no benefit to running with the ball if the final pass is wasted!*

Tip and Drill Number Fifty-Six: Running with the Ball Under Pressure

Drill fifty-five is a good option for learning to run with the ball at pace. However, having no opposition means that it is unrealistic for the match situation. This drill moves the previous one forward, introducing a chasing defender. (If, of course, the defender was to be in front of the runner, then the run turns into a dribble, with other skills applied).

The drill uses a similar space and method to the previous one.

Dribbling Aim: Run with the ball under pressure

Equipment: 30 m x 10m grid, with the narrow side divided into two channels. One ball per grid.

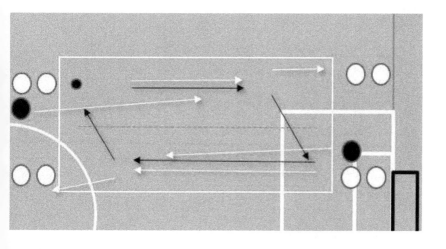

Method:

- *Minimum six players in three pairs, but several channels can be used at once.*
- *Two pairs at one end, one at the other in the opposite channel.*
- *Run with the ball at speed, using the laces to avoid breaking stride and pushing the ball approximately five meters ahead in a straight line. Partner gives a start set by the coach (a good starting point is setting the chaser off once the player touches the ball for the second time.)*
- *Ten meters from the end, make a diagonal pass into the adjacent channel for the next player to run back. Move into the opposite channel to wait for the next turn. Swap roles, so runner becomes defender, and vice versa.*

Key Skills (for runner):

- *Running as above.*
- *When defender closes, change body position to keep the ball protected.*
- *If necessary, because the defender is in a position to make a tackle, pass early or use the outside hook to buy time for the pass*

**Tip and Drill Number Fifty-Seven: Running with the Ball –
Advanced Drill**

This drill is best used with older or particularly able young players as it is a little complicated. However, it creates a scenario which is more realistic to the match situation.

Dribbling Aim: Run with the ball in busy scenario

Equipment: 40 m x 20 m grid, split in half lengthways (Block A and Block B). Four cones, one ball for each block.

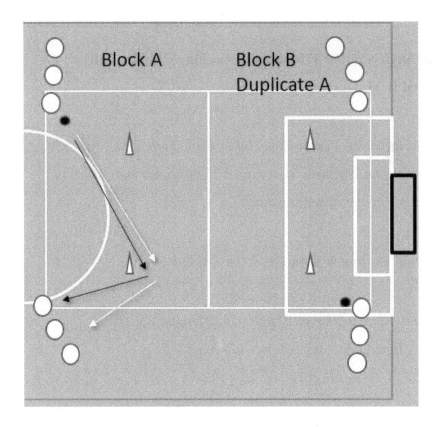

Method:

- *Twelve players. Six in each Block, three in each end corner of the block.*
- *Cones 5 meters from the center line, running at approximately 30 degrees from each corner.*
- *Player runs with the ball nearest to their teammates in the opposite corner of the block; the dribble round the cone*

and release a pass to the teammate in the opposite corner. Player continues run to new corner.

- *Add competitive element to see which Block, A or B, gets all their players to the opposite corner quickest.*

Key Skills (for runner):

- *Change speed at the turn.*
- *Ensure the pass at the end is accurate.*
- *Focus on the ball, the cone and teammates, ignore the noise from the other end of the grid.*

Tip and Drill Number Fifty-Eight: Parent Coaches

A little random, this tip, but worth making, nonetheless. In the previous chapter we highlighted the importance for the coach of spending equal time with all players, whatever their ability level.

Many coaches are also parents or close relatives of a member of the squad. This can be problematical for both the coach and their offspring. It is a good aim to treat one's own son or daughter exactly as others are treated. However, this is difficult. After all, we are parents before we are soccer coaches!

Further, the son or daughter is likely to be hypersensitive about being denied attention, or being singled out (and even more likely to be determined not to show this…) Other squad members will give undue weight to attention given to the child of the coach, even though this might be completely undeserved.

*It is a good idea not to coach one's own child, or brother or niece, but if this is difficult, it is probably wise to give a little less attention to our own child than that given to other players, but not overly so. Appearing unscrupulously fair in the perceptions of all (**which means being a little bit unfair to our own**) is the best way to avoid conflict. Whatever, it can be a tricky situation.*

Beating the Defender with a Change of Pace – The Old 'Knock and Go'

We are considering many tricky skills and techniques as aids to the work of the dribbler. However, one of the most effective is also one of the most straightforward. The 'knock and go' maybe has less use in youth soccer than with adults, because it is less likely that offside will be applied. It is a technique which is most effective when the ball is hit into space behind the defense, which has pushed up to create an offside trap. Used well, it can cause defenses to employ a sweeper system, which might negate the effectiveness of the knock and go but creates space in other ways.

Tip and Drill Number Fifty-Nine: Knock and Go in 1 v 1 games

Dribbling Aim: Use the knock and go to beat a player.

Equipment: 20 m x 10 m grid with small goal at each end.

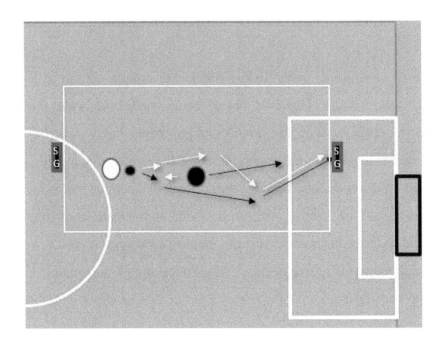

Method:

- *1 v 1.*
- *Aim is to pass the ball through a small 1m goal.*
- *Draw the defender in with close control at half pace.*
- *Knock the ball into the space created behind the defender.*
- *Sprint onto the ball.*
- *Utilize the space*

Key Skills:

- *When the player has been beaten, dribble across them as they chase back.*
- *Position body between defender and ball to prevent a tackle (a tackle from behind would result in a penalty and possible red card in a match).*
- *Keep arms wide to offer protection.*
- *In setting up 1 v 1 coach should try to match the pace of players as if one is vastly quicker the drill is less effective.*

Tip and Drill Number Sixty: Knock and Go Tactics

This drill is primarily focused on team play, with runs made by teammates creating space and opportunity for knock and go tactics.

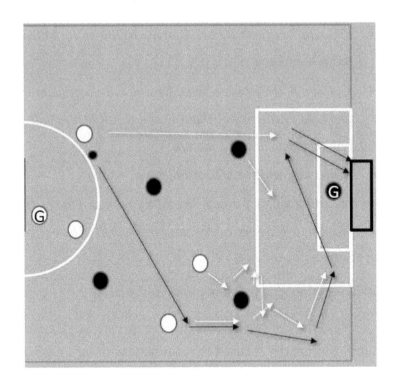

Dribbling Aim: Tactical Moves off the Ball.

Equipment: Small sided game.

Method:

- *5 v 5 up to 8 v 8.*
- *Encourage the center forward to get wide to make a 2 v 1 on the opposing full back.*
- *Team moves the ball to the winger.*

- *Center forward makes a diagonal run in behind the full back, forcing this player to move in to cover the pass.*
- *Winger knocks the ball long, exposing the space now created.*

Key Skills: (When to play the knock and go)

- *Communication of move.*
- *Seek to move the ball quickly once the full back is beaten to utilize the space before it is closed down.*

Tip and Drill Number Sixty-One: Running with the Ball

Coaches can advise their wingers to try a knock and go against full backs early in the game. **This way they can assess their players' speed against the defense.** In addition, opposing coaches might push their own defense deeper if they suspect the other side will seek to use speed to get in behind their own set up. This will create more space in midfield.

There are some enormous prizes in soccer. Winning your nation's principle cup competition, or the league championship are among the leading club competitions to which a professional can aspire. Even higher than these are victory in Europe, or South America; your continent's championship and, of course, the ultimate – winning the World Cup.

Individual prizes proliferate as well. Everything from man of the match (or its women's soccer equivalent) to the Ballon D'Or, especially now the twin hegemony of Ronaldo and Messi seems to be coming to an end.

Perhaps, though, the longest lasting, most durable achievement is to have a soccer move named after you. In this chapter, we look at some of the best and explore ways to integrate these tricks into the arsenal of the dribbler. Most of the drills in this chapter are individual ones, and do not tie in well with diagrams. However, numerous clips online exist for coaches who prefer to see a move in action before coaching it. Simply log the name of the move into a search engine, such as Google.

Tip and Drill Number Sixty-Two: Ronaldo Turn – Steps in Warm ups

Having just mentioned the great Portuguese wizard, here are two drills and a tip for working on the disguised drag back which is now known as the Ronaldo Turn (although, it is sometimes called the Okocha Turn, after the talented Nigerian attacking midfielder, Jay-Jay Okocha).

This drill practices the kind of ball manipulation required for the turn to be employed. It fits neatly into a simple 3 v 1 warm up passing routine.

Dribbling Aim: Passing warm up utilizing change of angle with ball manipulation

Equipment: 10 m x 10 m grid. One ball per grid.

Method:

- *Four players in a 3 v 1 rondo passing warm up.*
- *Players pass the ball within the grid, while the defender attempts to win possession.*
- *When possession is won, or the ball leaves the grid, the defender swaps role with the last player to touch the ball.*
- *Players change direction and create space using a drag back. The sole of the boot drags the ball sideways across*

*the body. The other foot dummies a pass in the other
direction.*

- *Player turns quickly in the direction of the ball, utilizing
the time and space created.*

Key Skills (for runner):

- *Disguise the move as much as possible.*
- *Accelerate onto the ball before passing (or dribbling).*

**Tip and Drill Number Sixty-Three: Ronaldo Turn in an Auckland
Square**

This simple drill can be used for any individual skill practice. It is
fast paced, requires good attention from players and includes an element
of pressure as the square is very busy. The drill is developed from a
popular rugby union training idea.

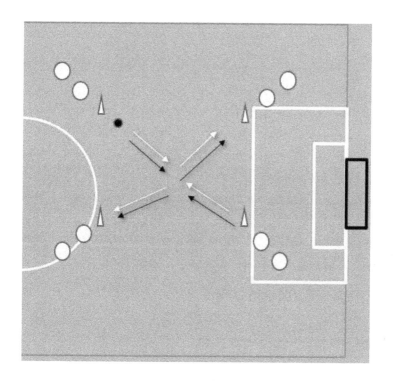

Dribbling Aim: Run with the ball and use a Ronaldo Turn.

Equipment: Four cones making a 20 m square. Two balls.

Method:

- *At least 8 players, but many more can be involved.*
- *Players split equally between the cones.*
- *Play starts from two opposite corners.*

- *Players dribbled towards the middle. Once there they enact a Ronaldo turn rotating 90 degrees, then pass to the cone they are now facing.*
- *The drill is repeated.*

Key Skills (for runner):

- *Awareness of another player at the center of the grid.*
- *Accelerate onto the ball at the change of direction.*
- *Drop lower at the turn.*

Tip and Drill Number Sixty-Four: Independent Practice

Young players knock balls around all the time. When a new skill is taught, set a competition for the following week based on the skill. For example, with the Ronaldo Turn, who can complete a circuit of turns the quickest? Encourage players to practice in their own time during the week.

Tip and Drill Number Sixty-Five: The Marseille Turn (1)

The Marseille Turn is the name often used for a skill developed by that master magician, Zinedine Zidane in his time at the club. This drill breaks the move down into its three constituent parts, since all are slightly alien to natural movement in soccer. As with the suggestion above, encourage players to practice the skills in their own time, as they will only stay focused on the drill below for a short time.

Dribbling Aim: Develop the skills of the Marseille Turn

Equipment: One ball per player.

Method:

- *Practice Skill One: stopping the ball. Dribble five meters. Stop the ball with the studs. Dribble on. Repeat until the skill is embedded.*
- *Practice Skill Two: Turning. As the ball is stopped rotate the body over the ball a full 360 degrees. Dribble on and repeat.*
- *Skill Three: This time, as the player rotates on the ball, the other foot drags the ball with the studs, changing the angle of run by about 45 degrees. Rather than rotating the full 360 degrees, the player now accelerates after the ball in the direction it has been dragged.*

Key Skills (for runner):

- *Start slowly to embed the movements.*

- *Use arms for balance and protect against the tackle.*

- *Accelerate onto the ball when it changes direction.*

Tip and Drill Number Sixty-Six: The Marseille Turn (2)

Use the Marseille Turn in an Auckland Square. However, this time, players run directly across the square, straightening up the dribble after the move has been completed. Therefore, players run from corners next to each other, rather than at diagonally opposite corners.

Tip and Drill Number Sixty-Seven: The Cruyff Turn (1)

Cruyff played in a slower time, but for all that he was the master among masters. The Dutch side of the 1970s must surely have been the best never to win the World Cup. Its principle of total football is back in fashion with players turning up on all parts of the pitch, and the game is more enjoyable for this. So, there has never been a better time to include the Cruyff turn among the skills we teach to our young players.

The Cruyff turn achieves the same outcome as the outside hook; a 180-degree change in direction creates space for a dribble, pass or shot. We would recommend developing the skills slowly, in two parts – the exaggerated fake shot or pass, then the 180 degree drag back with the inside of the foot. Once the two parts have been embedded, we can move onto the individual drill below to practice the skill.

Dribbling Aim: Practice the Cruyff Turn. Peer evaluation.

Equipment: Set of three cones 10 m apart. One ball per set of cones.

Method:

- *Two players per set of cones.*
- *Players take it in turns to practice the skill. While waiting their turn, they peer coach their partner, focusing on the two skills – the fake shot and the turn.*
- *Player starts at first cone, runs to second cone, completes the turn, returns to first cone, completes the turn, runs to third cone, completes the turn and passes back to teammate.*
- *Completing the move:*
  - *At the turning point, slow and raise outside foot for a shot.*
  - *Plant the opposite foot firmly.*
  - *Raise opposite arm for balance and disguise.*
  - *Opponent should commit to blocking the shot, placing them off balance*

- o *As the foot approaches the ball for the fake shot, rotate it so that it points at the other foot.*
- o *Drag the ball back 180 degrees, dropping and rotating at the same time.*
- o *Accelerate into the space created.*

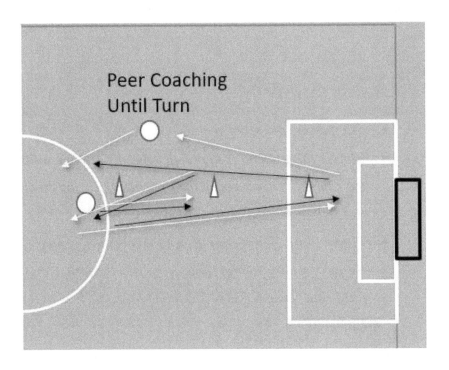

Key Skills (for the peer assessor):

- *Is the opposite arm raised?*
- *Is the fake shot apparent?*
- *Does the player rotate and accelerate into the turn?*

Tip and Drill Number Sixty-Eight: The Words of Johan Cruyff

*The great man's words can form the perfect mantra for young players. Youngsters love a motto (a fact frequently utilized by advertising firms!) and Cruyff's neatly combines the sort of clear message with verbal dexterity that young people love. **'Playing football (soccer) is simple. Playing simple football is the hardest thing in the world.'** In other words, keep it simple, but keeping it simple requires practice.*

Tip and Drill Number Sixty-Nine: La Costlyna

Carlos Costly isn't particularly (costly) as a player. The bulky Honduran striker is not a household name either, unlike those players mentioned above. But the little trick he developed is so simple, so effective that we have to include it. Again, we would suggest working with the group and demonstrating then practicing the elements of the move. Next encourage players to use it in warm up and matches.

Dribbling Aim: Learn the elements of La Costlyna.

Equipment: One ball per player.

Method:

- *Slow dribble to walking pace. The skill works as well by stopping the ball completely.*
- *Swing the outside foot, (The one, in a match, that would be furthest away from the defender) high above the ball as though about to play a back heel.*
- *Backheel over the ball (without making any contact) then immediately swing the foot forward, knock the ball on, and accelerate into the space created.*

Key Skills: (When to play La Costlyna)

- *The move works best in a wide position.*
- *The presence of a support player ready to receive a back heel makes the deceit more effective.*

Tip and Drill Number Seventy: The McGeady Spin

'Oh Aiden McGeady' they sing at Deepdale. (Now, there's a quiz question for soccer fans. Who play at Deepdale?) Indeed, the chant has been heard at various grounds which are not quite at the top of British soccer. Similarly, the Republic of Ireland international is a favourite when playing for his country.

The move he has immortalized is not dissimilar to the Marseille or Zidane turn, but is in fact quite different. It can be practiced in any of the cone track drills mentioned elsewhere in this book, or indeed as a part of any drill where space needs to be created. Once the elements have been learned, the following drill helps to practice it.

Dribbling Aim: Learn the elements of The McGeady Spin.

Equipment: One ball per player.

Method:

- *Attacker and semi passive defender*
- *Dribble away from the defender.*
- *Slow down when the defender is close, lower the body and put out arms for balance and protection.*
- *Hook the ball with the inside of the foot, stopping it and propelling it very slightly backwards.*
- *Rotate, and as a part of the rotation, complete the move with the outside of the other foot, pushing the ball further away from the defender. This will usually be at an angle of about 270 degrees*
- *Accelerate after the ball.*

Key Skills:

- *Remember to slow before the move.*
- *Do not hit the ball too hard with the initial, inside of the foot, contact.*

Tip and Drill Number Seventy-One: When to Use the McGeady Turn

*This particular move is most effective when the player in possession is being pressured by a **single defender approaching from behind**. Because the turn pushes the ball a fair distance from the foot, it is less effective in the close confines of midfield where the loose ball is likely to be picked up by a defender.*

Tip and Drill Number Seventy-Two: Warm Up Tip to Develop Individual Skills

A useful coaching tip is to have three or four simple passing warm ups that players know well. Then, throw in a secondary instruction to practice a specific turn. For example, the coach calls, 'Warm up, 3 v 1 passing, Ronaldo Turn'. Players then can quickly get warmed up whilst developing skills at the same time. We then encourage players to try out the skills in match situations.

Working on Your Weaker Foot

There are many reasons why most players tend to be one footed. The most scientific and therefore probably correct theory is to do, bizarrely enough, with the hand, and specifically how it is linked to language development. Linguists believe that as mankind acquired language, the hand was a very important tool in communication. Particularly the right hand (about 90 per cent of people are right-handed and right footed). The left side of the brain controls the right-hand side of the body's movements, and vice versa. While there appears to be no biological reason for the right side (and therefore left side of the brain) to be dominant, it is probable that humans with this sided dominance became more successful because of the development of their language. Thus, more of them were able to pass on their genes, and right handedness began to dominate.

Another theory argues that if both sides of the brain are equally dominant, humans develop in a way which leads to conflict in the brain over which side of the body will perform certain tasks. To avoid this conflict, man has evolved to have one side dominant.

The point of this brief and simplified biological lesson is that to attempt to turn a one-footed player into a two-footed player means challenging hundreds of thousands of years of evolution. And that, sadly, is probably beyond most soccer coaches.

In fact, most specialists in anatomy believe that there are virtually no genuine two footed, or two handed, sports players. Instead, whilst they have a dominant side, they are simply highly skilled with their weaker side, most probably as a result of practice.

Tip and Drill Number Seventy-Three: Annoy the Neighbors (using a wall)

The majority of drills in this book can be practised with the weaker foot used most. Coaches should encourage this a little, but players can quickly become frustrated and so the rule of little but often is a good one.

We can encourage children to practice with their weaker foot in their back yard, using a wall. Twenty repetitions of the following drill most days of the week will help young players to develop confidence in their weaker foot. It is important, though, to start young. Once players reach their teens it is very difficult to change habits.

Dribbling Aim: Develop confidence in the weaker foot.

Equipment: Home Drill. One ball and a wall needed. At least 10m of flat area to play on.

Method:

- *Start on the opposite side of the wall to the dominant foot. (So, right footed player starts on the left-hand side.)*
- *Play a gentle pass with the weaker foot, at 45 degrees, so it bounces off the wall towards the opposite side of the yard.*
- *Sprint laterally to intercept the wall pass at the other side of the wall.*
- *Control with the stronger foot and drag back with the weaker tone.*
- *Turn 180 degrees and close dribble with the weaker foot. Propel the ball with outside of the foot, making contact with the little toe.*
- *Throw in a skill – feint, step over, turn etc. – at halfway and continue to the starting point*
- *Step on the ball to stop it with the weaker foot, hook back with the stronger foot, and repeat the twenty times.*

Key Skills:

- *Dribble on toes.*
- *Pass with the instep.*
- *Vary the skill used at the halfway point of the dribble.*
- *Encourage players to be patient, it takes time to become comfortable with the weaker foot*

Tip and Drill Number Seventy-Four: Starting Young

One theory suggests that very young **children are naturally two footed and two handed**, *however as they reach the age of language competence, about four for most, they begin to favor one side as the opposite side of the brain becomes dominant. Parents can play a role in getting their children to develop equal (or near equal) dominance by playing with their children and keeping them using both feet for as long as possible, until a balance in strength between the feet becomes ingrained. Coaches can play a role by spreading the message to parents with younger children.*

Tip and Drill Number Seventy-Five: Tight Technical Skills with the Weaker Foot

Two simple drills to practice with the weaker foot in this section. Both are technical, and should be used regularly, but for no more than a couple of minutes (less with younger children) at a time and as a part of a general warm up routine.

Dribbling Aim: Two Weaker Foot Technical Skills to Develop Dexterity.

Equipment: One ball per player. Use as a part of a general warm up.

Method:

- *First Drill: Start with ball in front as per a normal dribbling position*
- *Roll the ball laterally with the studs of the stronger foot.*
- *Use the outside of weaker foot to move the ball slightly forwards at 45 degrees back towards its starting position.*
- *Step over the ball with the stronger foot, planting this foot firmly at the end of the step over, so the ball lies between and slightly in front of both feet.*
- *Sweep the ball slightly forward with the outside of the weaker foot.*

- *Advance three touches with the weaker foot, then repeat using the opposite foot.*
- *Repeat, increasing the speed of movement.*
- *Second Drill: Advance the ball with two touches of the inside of the weaker foot, then two with the outside.*
- *Stop the ball with the weaker foot (instep drag, outside of the foot drag or stepping on the ball) and drag it back.*
- *Turn 180 degrees and repeat the drill, speeding up.*

Key Skills:

- *Start slowly.*
- *Keep the body low, with arms out for balance.*
- *Accept failure – it is the first step towards success.*

Tip and Drill Number Seventy-Six: Two Footedness – Healthy Cynicism Towards the Myth

*There is a value to having good skills with the weaker foot, but in reality, there are relatively few occasions when the skill really becomes important. So, while we advocate working on the weaker foot, this should **never be to the detriment of the acquisition of other skills**.*

Dribbling and Shielding the Ball

It is true that the most exciting dribbling occurs when a player is flying down the wing, the full back laid low by a fantastic piece of skill, or a midfielder is driving through midfield. However, there will be time when a player receives the ball wide and is immediately under pressure. In this situation, the ball may need to be shielded until the player can turn and use a piece of skill to pass the defender or lay the ball off to a teammate.

Tip and Drill Number Seventy-Seven: Shielding in a Tight Space

A handy but tiring drill for keeping close possession of the ball in a tight space. It simulates the position whereby a dribbler is trapped in the corner.

Dribbling Aim: Shield the ball until an aggressive move can be made.

Equipment: Two 5 m x 5 m grids adjacent to each other. One ball per pair of grids.

Method:

- *Two attackers, one in each grid. One defender. Only the defender may cross into the other grid.*

- *Start with the ball in the corner of one of the grids, with the striker between the ball and the defender.*
- *Striker tries to shield the ball, while dribbling closely to create space for a clear dribble or pass.*
- *Once the dribbler has beaten the defender, he or she passes it into the other grid, where the defender tries to close down this striker.*
- *If the defender wins the ball, or it goes out of the grid, the defender swaps with the last striker to touch the ball.*
- *This is a tiring drill, and very physical, so should be played for no more than five minutes before a change.*

Key Skills (for the dribblers):

- *Position body sideways between the defender and the ball.*
- *Have arms out to maximize the distance between the defender and the ball.*
- *Keep the body low to allow for rapid changes of position and direction.*
- *Control the ball with small movements.*
- *Change direction often in an attempt to create some space from the defender.*
- *Use the sole of the foot and the outside of the foot furthest from the defender to control the ball and shift it around.*

- *When a small space is detected, perhaps the dribblers arm is no longer in contact with the defender, then try a piece of skill to beat the defender.*

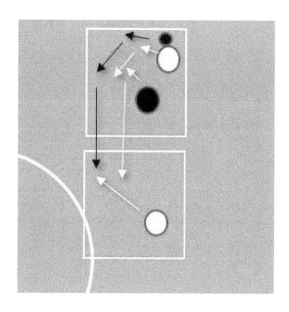

Tip and Drill Number Seventy-Eight: Developing Strength and Aggression

An aspect of the game to which young players sometimes take quickly, and sometimes do not, is the physical side of play. This simple drill is a good one to use with young players to get them used to this physical aspect. Since most youngsters love a wrestle, it is usually a popular one. It is, though, one of the very few drills we promote which does not use a ball.

Dribbling Aim: Develop confidence in the physical situation.

Equipment: Long white line.

Method:

- *Line the players up in pairs either side of the white line.*
- *Demonstrate legal contact – i.e. shoulder to shoulder.*
- *At the whistle players try to shoulder their opponents sideways so that they can cross the line.*

Key Coaching Points:

- *Monitor closely.*
- *Watch out for use of the hands to push a player illegally.*
- *Some youngsters find it very difficult to control their behavior in physical games such as this. Coaches should consider their players' temperaments before using this drill.*

Tip and Drill Number Seventy-Nine: Developing Strength and Aggression – Where Not to Go

A little philosophical consideration now. For every winner, there must be a loser. Being the loser all of the time is good for nobody, and coming absolutely is soul destroying, even if it is defended as being a 'part of life' or 'about growing up'. These are phrases usually used either by people who rarely experienced coming last or who have not thought through their words.

It seems a natural and fun development of the previous drill to increase competitiveness by extending the competition by eliminating losers until an overall winner is found, or by promoting winners forward until an overall champion emerges.

The second option is better than the first, in as much as there is no overall loser, just a group of them (!) but the question must be posed as to what these players gain watching their stronger (usually bigger) peers show off their physical prowess. The first option creates a last place – a horrible position in which to be in a physical contest.

*At the end of the day, **turning the shoulder drill into a strength contest delivers no useful results.** The winner risks relying on physicality rather than skill, whilst the loser is likely to have their confidence knocked.*

Drill seventy-eight is good for introducing physical contact, but it should stop there.

Tip and Drill Number Eighty: Kick it Out

This is a fun drill with young players attempting to kick other players' ball out of a grid, whilst retaining possession of their own. It helps to develop all round awareness in players.

Dribbling Aim: Learn to Protect the Ball in High Pressure Situations.

Equipment: 20 m x 20 m grid, one ball per player.

Method:

- *All players in the grid.*
- *Players attempt to keep their own ball safe, while kicking out the ball from other players.*
- *Once the ball is out, the player is out.*
- *Continue until only one player is left.*

Key Skills:

- *Keep all round awareness by using the head on a swivel technique.*
- *Protect the ball by keeping low, with knees bent and arms out.*
- *When approached, try to keep the body between player and ball.*
- *Make the decision when it is best to approach another player's ball, and when it is best to keep possession.*

Tip and Drill Number Eighty-One: Kick It Out Advanced.

This is the same drill as above, but by turning it into a team game, with one ball between two players, the game takes on a whole new set of additional challenges.

Players must develop communication skills; they need to develop a strategy, but also be flexible enough to change the strategy as the situation dictates.

The Nutmeg – Pushing the Ball Between the Defender's Legs

Everybody loves a nutmeg…except for the defender on the receiving end. In fact, the only thing likely to earn more hoots of derision than being nutmegged is to attempt one and fail. This chapter should help to address this potential humiliation for the striker, while making it a more likely event for the defense.

Tip and Drill Number Eighty-Two: The Nutmeg Warm Up

Here is another variation on Drill Eighty-One, kick it out. The same drill operates, but this time the players are divided into two teams. Now, when their ball is kicked out, they stand with their legs apart ready to be 'nutmegged' by a teammate.

Once this happens, they are back in the game. At the end of a specified time – 3 to 5 minutes is good - whichever team has the most 'active' players wins.

It is a fun drill but helps players to understand that the nutmeg requires precision, with the ball best played with the instep with knees bent and head over the ball.

Tip and Drill Number Eighty-Three: The Feint Nutmeg

The challenge for any player trying a nutmeg is to get their defender's legs to open wide enough to play the ball through. The following drills are interchangeable.

Dribbling Aim: The Fake Pass Nutmeg.

Equipment: Two cones to represent defender's legs, narrow channel 10 m x 3 m. One ball.

Method:

- *Up to six players, minimum three. Narrow channel with cones placed 2-3 meter apart in the middle. This can also be done individually*
- *Player dribbles slowly at cones.*
- *Dribbler makes an exaggerated fake pass.*
- *As defender stretches to block the pass (in the drill, the cones have been placed to represent this) the dribbler passes the ball through the legs with the instep of the foot, accelerates round the defender (cones) and repeats the move at the next set of cones. Using multiple sets encourages players to weight the nutmeg effectively.*

- *After the final nutmeg, the player passes the ball to the end of the channel.*
- *The next player repeats the exercise.*

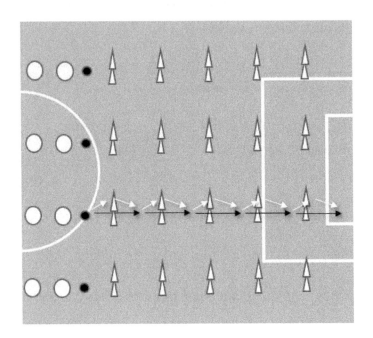

Key Skills:

- *Remember to disguise the fake pass with eyes and body.*
- *Decide early which way to make the fake pass, so you know which leg will stretch out to stop it.*

Tip and Drill Number Eighty-Four: Risky Nutmeg

The risk of failure with this nutmeg is high, However, when it comes off, the impact is great and the defense will be thrown by the move, creating space for the dribbler and his or her teammates.

Dribbling Aim: Perfect the nutmeg from a special trick.

Equipment: Half pitch, one ball, two cones.

Method:

- *One defender, one keeper, one striker.*
- *Cones represent the second defender.*
- *Defender begins on center of penalty area D and cannot move until the nutmeg is completed.*
- *Dribbler dribbles from center to wide at 45-degree angle. As the dribbler passes the cone defender, the ball is flicked with the instep of the outside foot, nutmegging the cones (defender).*
- *Dribbler accelerates round the cones, onto the ball and tries to finish the shot (see final chapter for techniques)*
- *Defender and keeper try to prevent the goal.*

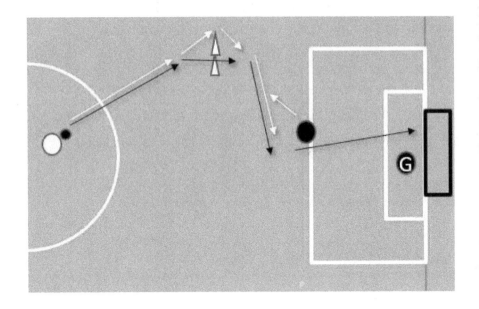

Key Skills:

- *Remember to slow before the nutmeg.*
- *Consider how best to deal with the onrushing defender.*

Tip and Drill Number Eighty-Five: The Step Over and Poke

This drill employs the Auckland Square demonstrated earlier in the book (see Drill 63).

Dribbling Aim: Practice another form of the Nutmeg under pressure.

Equipment: Four cones surrounding a 20 m square. Two balls.

Method:

- *Players split equally between the four cones. At least two on each cone.*
- *Players from two sides of the square dribble towards the center of the square.*
- *Defenders from the opposite corner come to meet them.*
- *Dribbler performs a stepover with one foot, then pokes the ball through the legs of the defender with the outsides of the other foot.*
- *Dribbler moves past the defender and passes to the corner to which they are running. Drill is repeated.*
- *Dribblers should vary the foot with which they perform the step over.*

Key Skills:

- *Be aware of other players in the middle.*
- *Keep low, knees bent and arms for balance at the delivery of the skill.*
- *Defenders must 'buy' the step over.*

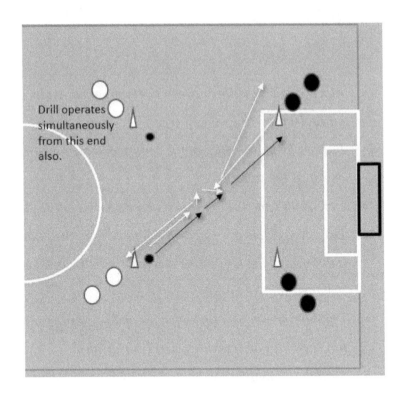

Drill operates
simultaneously
from this end
also.

Tip and Drill Number Eighty-Six: Don't Let Success Go to Your Head!

Completing a nutmeg gives a great buzz to a player. Repeating it is amazing. Trying it a third time is a sign of success going to a player's head. Unwise at any time! And definitely a lesson young player needs to learn.

Dribble and Shoot

It is certainly true that dribbling can be effective at any part of the pitch. The keeper beating an onrushing striker hoping to close her down and ruin her distribution; a full back charging down the wing to launch an attack and so on. However, it is dribbling that leads to goals that really excites the fans and offers them the biggest thrill.

Therefore, in the last two chapters, we will look at dribbling leading to goal scoring situations. As before, most of the drills are interchangeable and can be used for whichever finish is being practised.

Tip and Drill Number Eighty-Seven: Making Space on the Stronger Foot

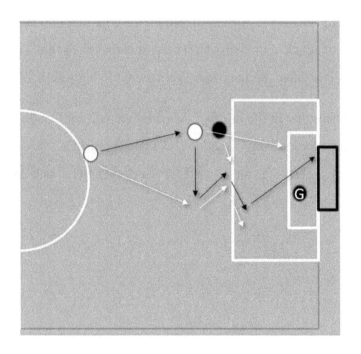

Dribbling Aim: Dribble and shoot with the stronger foot.

Equipment: Half pitch, one ball.

Method:

- *Dribbler, target man, defender, keeper. Defender starts behind the target man, who is facing his own team. If the defender is not tight to the target man, he or she can turn and shoot themselves.*

- *Dribbler lays ball into target man, and moves forward onto their stronger side (e.g., right footer to right side).*
- *Target man lays the ball off. Defender closes down.*
- *Dribbler uses a skill to shift the ball away from the defender and create space outside of them.*
- *Dribbler shoots, target man chases in any rebounds.*

Key Skills:

- *Create space onto stronger foot*
- *Shoot across the goal.*

Tip and Drill Number Eighty-Eight: Shooting off the Weaker Foot

Dribbling Aim: Hit with power and accuracy after a run.

Equipment: Three balls, agility ladder, cones.

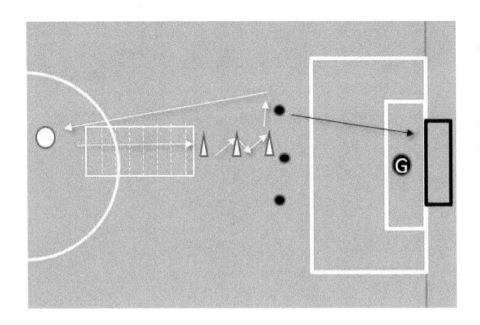

Method:

- *One attacker, one keeper.*
- *Balls laid level with edge of the D, one central, one to the right, one to the left.*
- *Striker must run through the ladder, weave through the cones (simulating dribbling techniques) and shoot.*
- *After each shot the player repeats the routine until all shots have been completed.*
- *Striker can choose the order in which they shoot, but only one shot is permitted with the stronger foot.*

Key Skills:

- *Focus on running at pace through the agility obstacles.*
- *Position to run onto the ball.*

Tip and Drill Number Eighty-Nine: The Curler

An advanced drill here, which includes a number of the skills worked on already. We have described the drill as it might be used with beginners. As players advance the drill is developed firstly by replacing the mannequins with real defenders, then by turning the drill into a 5 v 3 rondo practice.

Dribbling Aim: Create opportunities for the curler

Equipment: Half pitch.

Method:

- *3 v 2 mannequines plus keeper.*
- *The attacker switch the play and create a 2 v 1 on the wing.*
- *Player in possession cuts back using a turn, and plays the ball to the support player.*

- *Receiver is on 'wrong' wing, for example, a right footer on the left side.*
- *Receiver lets the ball across their body and touches it on with the stronger foot.*
- *Now the body is perfectly placed to curl a shot towards the far corner, using the defender as a shield to obscure the keeper's view.*

Key Skills:

- *On cutting inside, the ball will be in a perfect position for a first-time strike, so shoot early.*

Tip and Drill Number Ninety: The Poke Between Defenders

Poking the ball between two closing defenders is a risky move, but one which can deliver great rewards. Not only are two players taken out of the game by the dribbler's skill, but a mis-timed challenge can result in a free kick or penalty.

Dribbling Aim: Poke the ball between defenders to win a penalty or have a shot on goal.

Equipment: Two mannequins, one ball.

Method:

- *Two dribblers, keeper. Note this drill can replace mannequins with real defenders, but there is a risk of injury if the timing of tackles is not precise.*
- *First dribbler accelerates down wing.*
- *Passes into second dribbler, who pokes the ball between mannequins, and hops between them.*
- *This dribbler then attempts to score.*

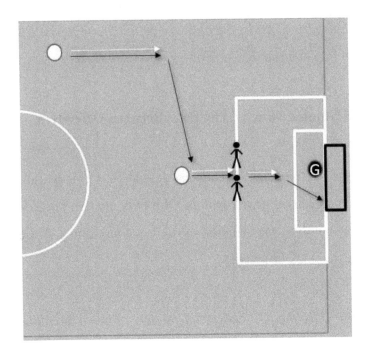

Key Skills:

- *Regain balance after hop, and side foot shot past keeper.*

Tip and Drill Number Ninety-One: Driving for Deflection

This is a 5 v 3 + keeper rondo game.

Dribbling Aim: Shoot hard and low to increase the chance of deflection.

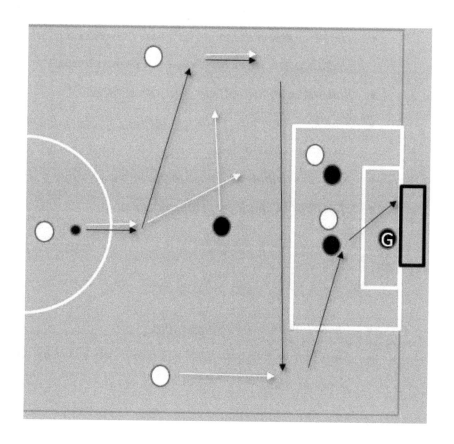

Equipment: Half pitch.

Method:

- Five attackers. Two must remain in penalty area for defections. The other three are spread across the pitch and can travel anywhere.

- Three defenders. Two must remain in the penalty area, as must the keeper. The other defender can go anywhere.

- *The three free moving strikers may only pass the ball ONCE each – they can choose not to pass at all.*
- *Ball starts on the halfway line with a striker.*
- *Attackers advance, at some stage the free defender must commit to close down.*
- *Attackers dribble and pass to get into a shooting position.*
- *Shot must be made from outside the area.*

Key Skills:

- *Shoot low with the stronger foot.*
- *Shift ball to side with final touch to create the room for a powerful shot.*

Tip and Drill Number Ninety-Two: Opening Up the Body

As we alluded to earlier, anybody who watched the French superstar of football, Thierry Henry, will know of the power of opening up the body and shooting across the goal.

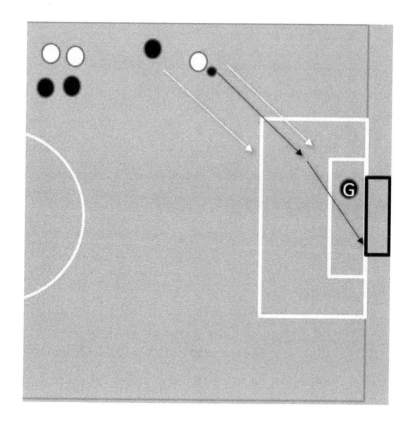

Dribbling Aim: Open up the body to shoot low.

Equipment: Half pitch or 30 m x 20 m grid. One ball.

Method:

- *Attacker starts wide on the opposite side to their stronger foot.*
- *Defender begins 2 meters behind striker.*

- *Striker runs at pace into the angle of the area.*
- *Striker opens up chest, so it is point directly towards the opposite side of the penalty area.*
- *Striker shoots with the instep of the stronger foot, firmly but smoothly, aiming low just outside the far post. This takes it away from the keeper and it should curl back inside the post.*
- *Next pair go, and on next turn roles are swapped.*

Key Skills:

- *When running with the ball keep the body between ball and defender, with arms out, to protect the ball.*
- *Keep the non-kicking foot planted firmly, until the change in balance on shooting causes the striker to fall away. Spreading the arms prevents this for as long as possible.*

Tip and Drill Number Ninety-Three: The Importance of End Product

*It is very important to stress to players that dribbling **must have an end product**. It might be a pass or a shot, but it has not been successful if it has not created an opportunity for an attack.*

Dribble Round the Keeper

The drills for this final set of skills can be very similar, with a dribble from various angles against a keeper.

Pressure can be added by including a defender coming from behind. In this case, the striker should always look to keep their body between the ball and the onrushing defender. They should also angle their run across them to stop a sliding tackle from the side. Tackling from behind is illegal even if successful and will result in a penalty and possible red card.

The diagram below is a standard set up which can be adapted to each of the drills below. Prior to setting up the drill a demonstration from the coach will make the technique clearer.

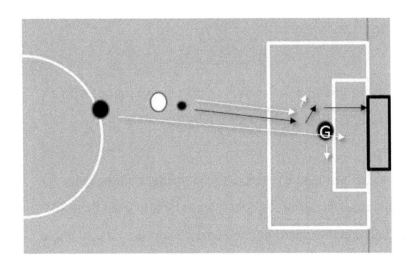

Tip and Drill Number Ninety-Four: One v One straight on

Specific Aims: Shoot before the keeper is set, keep the shot low.

Method:

- *Slow down as the edge of the area is reached to steady oneself for the shot.*
- *Head over the ball when shooting to keep the ball low.*
- *Place the shot with the instep aiming for the corner.*
- *Hook the ball with the inside of the foot, stopping it and propelling it very slightly backwards.*
- *It is harder to round the keeper when running straight at the goal, as there is no wide space in which to head.*

Key Skills:

- *Use eyes to fool the keeper.*
- *Use a head swivel as you slow to check for closing defenders and support attackers.*

Tip and Drill Number Ninety-Five: One v One from an angle

It is harder to score with a direct shot when dribbling from wide. Rounding the keeper becomes a more viable option in this situation.

Dribbling Aim: Dummy the keeper to find space.

Method:

- *Drive quickly to the edge of the box to give as much time as possible.*
- *Option: open the body as if to shoot, drag the ball back using the instep and push forward with the instep of the other foot, taking the ball round the narrow side of the keeper as he or she dives to cover the shot to the far post. OR.*

- *Use the outside of the foot – right foot from left side and vice versa – to pull the ball back at right angles into the space away from the keeper.*
- *Chip over the keeper's diving body or take a second touch with the outside of the same boot to take the ball away from the keeper.*

Key Skills:

- *Use eyes to sell the dummy.*
- *Use head swivel to check for arriving defenders or teammates.*

Tip and Drill Number Ninety-Six: The early shot

Sometimes an early shot from outside the box can catch the keeper unawares. Again, disguise is a key skill.

Dribbling Aim: Shoot early to catch out the keeper

Method:

- *This method works best from a straightish run.*

- *Run fast with the ball.*
- *Hit the ball first time without shifting it sideways. Shoot from outside the box.*
- *Drive through the ball with the laces.*
- *Keep head over the ball to keep the shot low.*

Key Skills:

- *Give as little indication to the keeper that a shot is coming to catch them by surprise.*
- *Follow in the shot for rebounds.*

Tip and Drill Number Ninety-Seven: The Chip

The chip is often a spectacular finish but can also evoke criticism when it fails. However, it is an important skill, one child love to practice, and they should be encouraged to express themselves with this move.

Dribbling Aim: Put the keeper on the floor, then chip to score.

Method:

- *Slow the dribble and bring the ball under closer control as the edge of the box is reached.*

- *As the keeper closes, employ one of the skills outlined earlier to sell a dummy, such as a feint, step over, turn or drag back.*

- *As the keeper commits, use the outside of the chipping foot to push the ball laterally away from the keeper.*

- *Move onto the ball, and as the keeper hits the floor, chip the ball with moderate force and good control to get height to clear the keeper, but not so much that the ball goes over the bar.*

Key Skills (Of the Chip):

- *Ensure approach to the ball is at a slight angle (it should be, following the dummy).*

- *Place the non-kicking foot about four to six inches away from and slightly behind the ball.*

- *Take a short backswing with the kicking foot.*

- *As the foot comes back to chip the ball, angle the toe downwards to make a wedge shape, getting the foot under the ball.*

- *Lean back as the kick takes place.*

Tip and Drill Number Ninety-Eight: Dribbling in Space at the Keeper

This final drill is closer to match play and allows the dribbler practice different techniques finish a 1 v 1 with the keeper.

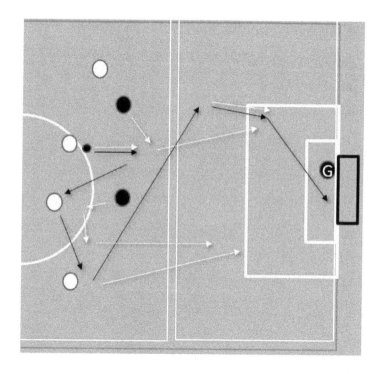

Dribbling Aim: Create space for a through pass for a 1 v 1, finish the move by beating the keeper.

Equipment: Half pitch divide into two width ways.

Method:

- *Four attackers, two defenders and a keeper.*
- *The keeper apart, all players start in the zone furthest from the goal. They can only leave this zone once the ball has been passed or dribbled into the final zone.*
- *Keeper starts on goal line. Although false, this creates more opportunity for the 1 v 1 to materialize, particularly on a small junior pitch.*
- *Four players pass the ball to create space for a through ball for a team mate to run on to.*
- *Timing the pass correctly will give the runner an advantage over the defense, creating a 1 v 1 with keeper, but one in which there is pressure.*
- *Dribbler attempts to score; other attackers support and defense tries to cover back.*
- *Dribbler uses a skill to score a goal.*

Key Skills:

- *Angle the through ball to prevent the keeper from running out and clearing up.*
- *Supporting players communicate defense and support.*

Tip and Drill Number Ninety-Nine: Is it Best to Shoot or Dribble?

Statistically, it is usually best to shoot. The only times this might not be the best option is when the dribbler is coming from wide – too wide to open the body and shoot, or where this would involve using the weaker foot and the striker is not confident of doing this. Or when the dribbler has lost control, and the ball comes too close to the keeper to allow a shot.

Beating the keeper with a dribble slows down the move, giving more time for defenders to cover; a good keeper is also able to cover a surprisingly large area when diving.

However, the skill is an important one for players to acquire. And, it is great fun to try out!

Conclusion

We cannot stress enough the importance of dribbling in soccer. It is a skill which brings the unexpected to a game, unlocks defenses by forcing them out of their structural comfort zone. It is thrilling to watch.

Drilling into young players the idea that not every dribble will work is very important. Players must develop the mental strength to experiment and try out their skills, overcome inevitable failures. If, as coaches, we instil too strict a game plan, take decision making away from our young performers, we limit their development.

So, we say to every young player, and urge their coaches to do the same…

Tip and Drill Number One Hundred: Just Do It!

Soccer is a game meant for entertainment. OK, so the chances are we won't be playing, or coaching, in front of crowds of 50000 cheering fans, but there might be a handful on the touchline. On top of that, there are the other twenty-one players, the subs and, most importantly, ourselves to whom we can bring cheer. There are certain elements of soccer which give a thrill more than any other:

- The screamer which flies into the top corner, making the net bulge.
- The shot which crashes off the bar.
- The defence splitting pass which turns soccer from a sport into an art form.
- The thrilling, sliding tackle (enjoy it before it is totally eliminated from the game).
- The diving header (see above!!!).
- The full length, diving save.
- The goal mouth scramble…

Certainly, among the most exciting of this list of 'high points', and some would argue sitting proudly on the top, is the dribble. Whether it is a powerful surge through midfield, defenders desperately trying to keep up, or the piece of individual brilliance, the skill which beats a player and creates sudden, gaping space, the dribble is a part of the game that pushes people onto the edges of their seats. Metaphorically and literally.

But we cannot deliver that thrill if we do not *attempt to dribble the ball.* And if it does not come off? Well, we can still be sure the sun will rise tomorrow.